THE LITTLE

# Restorative Justice for Sexual Abuse

## Hope through Trauma

# JUDAH OUDSHOORN

With
Lorraine Stutzman Amstutz
Michelle Jackett

Good Books
New York, New York

Library of Congress Cataloging-in-Publication Data is available on file.

ISBN: 978-1-68099-055-3
e-ISBN:978-1-68099-116-1

Printed in the United States of America

**The Little Books of Justice & Peacebuilding** present, in highly accessible form, key concepts and practices from the fields of restorative justice, conflict transformation, and peacebuilding. Written by leaders in these fields, they are designed for practitioners, students, and anyone interested in justice, peace, and conflict resolution.

**The Little Books of Justice & Peacebuilding** series is a cooperative effort between the Center for Justice and Peacebuilding of Eastern Mennonite University and publisher Good Books.

# Table of Contents

1

# Introduction

*A* girl is sexually abused by her stepfather. How can we help?

A man is arrested for soliciting sex from a minor. What can we do to make sure it doesn't happen again?

A teenage boy is sexually assaulted by his youth pastor. How can a faith community respond?

An indigenous community is devastated by sexual abuse. How does it heal?

This book considers the use of restorative justice in response to sexual abuse. How might such interventions address the above situations?

Restorative justice is gaining increasing acceptance for addressing harm and crime. Interventions have been developed for a wide range of wrongdoing. Rather than a blueprint or a specific set of programs, restorative justice is about mapping possibilities. Because it is not prescriptive, it gives communities more flexibility, more power in responding to violent crimes like sexual abuse. Restorative justice is concerned with the disproportionate attention given to offenders, often at the expense of victims; it seeks to balance concerns for both those who have been harmed and those who have caused harm.

This book asks the following questions:

1.  What can a restorative justice approach offer to people who are victims of sexual abuse, people who have offended sexually, and communities impacted by sexual violence?
2.  How does restorative justice complement or differ from what is already being done by the therapeutic and legal communities?
3.  How can we create communities where victims are supported, offenders are accountable, and all can live safely?
4.  What would it mean, philosophically and practically, to shift some justice resources from enforcement, courts, and prisons toward prevention and the needs of the people who have been harmed?
5.  How can restorative justice address structural violence—such as patriarchy, racism, and colonialism—when responding to sexual abuse?

# What is this book about?

**This book is *not* about making excuses for offenders.** Sexual abuse is wrong. When a person chooses to sexually offend against another, he or she causes tremendous harm not only to direct victims but also to others in the community. Regardless of offenders' own histories—which often include hurt and/or trauma—they need to be accountable for their choices. Restorative justice does not minimize harm, make excuses, or help offenders avoid consequences. Sometimes people equate restorative justice with forgiveness and/or reconciliation. These are not priorities of restorative justice, unless desired by those harmed. Restorative justice takes a stand against violence, for community safety.

**This book *is* about moving victim needs to the forefront.** Most of the financial and human resources of criminal justice machinery are spent on offenders. From policing to courts to prisons, North America dispenses billions of dollars on those who have caused criminal harm. This is often at the expense of meeting the needs of victims. Conversely, restorative justice starts by asking, "Who has been hurt?" followed by "What do they need?" This fundamentally moves victim needs to the forefront. The majority of victims do not disclose their experiences of sexual abuse. North America needs a justice framework that starts by believing victims. Many are afraid of being doubted, ridiculed, and/or blamed. Restorative justice practices should start by believing victims, establishing safety for them, and prioritizing their healing.

**This book is *not* a soft- or a tough-on-crime approach.** Some assume that restorative justice allows people to take the easy way out, to avoid jail time or punishment. Others argue that it is actually more demanding than conventional punishment. In reality, restorative justice is multi-faceted. It considers how to repair harm when needs are different, or even in opposition to each other. Consider the predicament: many people in a society want those who have offended sexually to suffer for their wrongdoing, while others who have been hurt simply want acknowledgement and changed behavior from an offender. Soft-on-crime ("hug-a-thug") tends to minimize harm, while tough-on-crime ("lock 'em up and throw away the key" or "tail 'em, nail 'em, jail 'em") minimizes real accountability. Both approaches sideline the complex needs of victims.

That being said, prison and restorative justice are not mutually exclusive. Prisons can be an important part of community safety—at least temporarily. When a person is unsafe to him- or herself or others, incapacitation is vital. Yet longer sentences or punishment for punishment's sake (or political expediency) often do not make our communities safer, nor do they always satisfy victims. Although some prison rehabilitative programs have proven effective for offenders, the overuse of imprisonment alone has often made communities less safe. For victims, arrest and conviction can provide some vindication, but the process itself is often re-traumatizing and does not go far enough to meet their needs.

**This book *is* smart on crime and/or harm.** Restorative justice is comprehensive, asking intelligent questions of those affected by harm. Healthy restorative justice practices consider victim trauma and offender accountability as well community safety. "Smart on crime" means interventions must also be geared toward preventing future harms. Smart on crime means not being silent about sexual abuse.

**This book** *acknowledges* **sexual abuse as a form of gender-based violence.** While both men and women perpetrate violence, the majority of sexual offenders are men. This book is not anti-men, nor does it suggest that men are prone to being rapists. However, sexual abuse is predominately a male-perpetuated issue. The restorative justice framework described in this book acknowledges that sexual abuse is a form of gender-based violence. While some women also perpetrate sexual abuse—and this should not be forgotten, especially for their victims—sexual abuse will not be eradicated until more men stand up to challenge the forms of masculinity that perpetuate it. As authors, we are indebted to many scholars and practitioners concerned with gender issues who have championed, often at great personal cost, an end to gender-based violence.

**This book** *acknowledges* **that racism and colonialism in North American criminal justice systems have been very harmful toward particular people groups, namely African American, Latino, and indigenous peoples.** Restorative justice practices must be careful not to ignore or perpetuate racial inequality. Criminal justice systems have been used as a tool by white men to maintain power over other races: to marginalize and colonize. White supremacy needs to be challenged. In the case study of the Ojibwe people of Hollow Water (later in the book), we will highlight how structural or collective violence, like colonialism and racism, are connected to individual violence, including sexual abuse.

**This book** *acknowledges* **community as a value.** Restorative justice is about people. It is about people

5

learning to live together in a way that honors the dignity of all. Respect for all means talking about harm and supporting those who are hurt. It also means that sex offenders are people, too. They are fathers and stepfathers, mothers and stepmothers, uncles and aunts, cousins, brothers and sisters. People hurt each other for a variety of reasons. It is important that offenders have support, alongside accountability, to heal and understand their choices.

A restorative justice framework suggests that accountability happens best when people are supported. Eileen Henderson, Restorative Justice Manager of Mennonite Central Committee Ontario, observes, "Reintegration is a myth when most offenders were never integrated to start with." This is not an excuse, minimizing the harm they have chosen to perpetrate, but a reality that offenders need space to heal and develop healthy relationships. Communities include people who have been hurt, people who have caused harm, and people who have both harmed and are hurting. Restorative justice values all members of a community.

**This book does *not* advocate specific programs, including those based on face-to-face dialogue.** People often equate restorative justice with encounter, a face-to-face meeting between victim and offender. While such approaches may be appropriate or desirable in some cases, there are many situations where this type of dialogue is not advisable. Sometimes offenders are unwilling to take the responsibility demanded by an encounter-based restorative justice program and/or would not willingly participate. Moreover, many victims do not need, or want, to meet with the person who caused them harm. Most significantly, most perpetrators of sexual abuse are not caught. If dialogue is the only restorative justice tool available, this approach will miss the majority of victims and offenders. Restorative justice is first and foremost a framework, a way of doing justice. Only secondarily is it a type of program.

**This book *is* but one framework.** There is much work to do in supporting victims of sexual abuse and holding offenders accountable. Restorative justice offers some pieces, but not all, in the puzzle to accomplish this. Furthermore, as restorative justice advocate Howard Zehr notes, we are still early on the learning curve of doing and articulating restorative justice. Practitioners must be open to critique and change while also being careful about over-promising what they can do. The framework in this book can coexist or be in partnership with others. For example, criminal justice processes are exactly what some victims and offenders need. Rule of law, due process, public denunciation of wrong, and the protection of rights are important elements of justice and community safety. In fact, in Canada and some parts of the United States, citizens have a legal obligation to report any abuse of children to the appropriate authorities. Too many times, people running institutions have covered up sexual abuse, trying to handle it on their own, only causing further harm. Furthermore, therapeutic models are an important part of healing for both victims and offenders. Remembering, mourning, and reconnecting through these processes are vital steps for victim recovery.[1] Cognitive behavioral therapy and relapse prevention models have proven to be excellent ways of helping many offenders to avoid reoffending.

This book is an invitation to further respectful dialogue. It is conversational rather than prescriptive or confrontational.

**This *is* a tough issue.** Many people have been hurt by sexual abuse. And many of these people have

7

also been further traumatized by how people have responded to it—from family members doubting their stories to a criminal justice system that challenges their facts, their truth about what happened. We as authors acknowledge this. We tread into these waters with caution and utmost respect for those who have survived sexual abuse.

## Why this book?

This book was written because of the urgency of the issues it addresses, and because so many have asked what restorative justice has to say to sexual offending and harm. We would like to highlight two specific concerns:

1.  **The need for safe communities.** The heart of this book is about creating safe communities. In the next chapter, we will discuss the widespread nature of sexual abuse. More needs to be done to acknowledge and end it.

2.  **The need for imaginative conversations.** Our society's intervention methods to date are limited at best. This is true of both criminal and restorative justice. Our hope is that this book sparks the imagination of the reader to try new, safe, creative ways of addressing the harm of sexual abuse.

## Book outline:

*   Chapter 2 describes the issue of sexual abuse, its impact on victims, and why some offenders perpetrate it.

- Chapter 3 describes a restorative justice framework.
- Chapter 4 uses a case study to describe how a restorative justice framework can be used with victims.
- Chapter 5 uses a case study to describe how a restorative justice framework can be used with offenders.
- Chapter 6 uses a case study to describe how a restorative justice framework can be used within communities (our example is a faith community).
- Chapter 7 describes the way the Ojibwe people of Hollow Water First Nation responded to epidemic sexual abuse, using indigenous healing circles to heal victims, offenders, and the community.
- Chapter 8 describes some limits and possibilities of restorative justice based on academic literature on the topic.
- Chapter 9 describes principles that can guide restorative practice in cases of sexual violence.
- Chapter 10 concludes with a case story.

# Integrity

Many emphasize restorative justice as a values-based approach. In this book, we would like to highlight integrity as a key value. Restorative justice, from our perspective, is a pursuit of wholeness: wholeness of individuals and communities. If we facilitate restorative justice dialogue between victims and offenders without addressing root causes, we only accomplish justice in part. If we encourage others to be accountable for their actions without holding ourselves to the same standard, justice is partial. If we work to repair relationships in communities while failing to work respectfully with all people and systems, integrity is compromised. In the hope of addressing all of these problems, restorative justice is motivated by and strives toward integrity.

## A note on terminology

Increasingly, the labels "victim" and "offender" are being reevaluated. While these terms provide convenient shorthand references and are common within the criminal justice system, they also tend to oversimplify and stereotype—people are much more than what they have done or experienced. In criminology, labeling theory has emphasized that labels are judgmental, and people may tend to become what they are labeled.

We see no good alternative to using these terms, but we urge you to keep these concerns in mind.

2

# Understanding Sexual Abuse

I n this chapter we define the terms "sexual abuse," "victim," and "offender." We discuss the impacts of sexual abuse on victims and introduce a few concepts related to sexual offending. This will provide the backdrop for explaining how restorative justice can respond.

## Sexual abuse

Sexual abuse is any unwanted, nonconsensual, attempted, or completed sexual contact, perpetrated by an offender against someone. It includes rape, sexual assault, incest, molestation, sexual harassment, inappropriate touch, indecent exposure, and child pornography. Although the contact is described as sexual, it is better understood as violence because it is a violation of the sexual integrity of one human being by another. Sexual abuse causes harm to victims, offenders, and communities. It is typically experienced as a trauma by the victim and may be so overwhelming that the person does not know whether she or he will survive. For some, sexual abuse becomes a part of their "normal" lives as they are consistently violated by a family member or loved one. Mending from this can also be highly traumatic. (For more information about trauma and how it affects the brain, see Carolyn Yoder's *The Little Book of Trauma Healing*.)

It is estimated that 1 in 3 women and 1 in 6 men will experience some form of sexual abuse in their lifetime.[2]

## Victims

As noted earlier, language—and specifically labels—can be problematic. It is important for people who have experienced sexual abuse to be able to tell their stories—in ways *they* understand it, including how to define their experience. Some might prefer to be called "victims," others "survivors" or even "thrivers." For the purpose of this book, we will use the term "victim," as it indicates that something harmful and uncontrollable has been done to someone without his or her consent. Using "victims" allows us to say that what happened to these individuals was not chosen, nor their fault. It was imposed: a violation. However, a caution with this term is that victims do not necessarily remain helpless or permanently entrapped in their victimhood. Often others want to tell victims how to respond, which is not helpful. However, when choices or processes of resilience are made available to victims, they are better able to take steps toward healing.

# Offenders

A person who has offended sexually is someone who has done something monstrous, but he or she is not a monster inherently. The action of sexual offending is named as harmful and wrong. However, the person who perpetrated it should not be dehumanized in spite of the fact that he or she has treated a victim in a dehumanizing way. Sexual offending does not represent the full humanity of the person who perpetrated it. In Community Justice Initiatives (Kitchener, Canada), a man in a peer support group for people who have offended sexually said, "Once people started to treat me like a human being, I realized I better start acting like one." The value of distinguishing the offense from the person is that it allows for the person to heal, while also holding him or her accountable for harmful choices. This way of viewing offenders is important for community safety, as will be discussed in chapter 5. For the sake of simplicity, we will use the term "offender" to represent people who have offended sexually.

## A sexual offense cycle

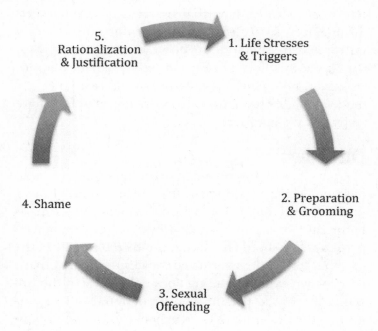

5. Rationalization & Justification

1. Life Stresses & Triggers

4. Shame

2. Preparation & Grooming

3. Sexual Offending

## The sexual abuse cycle

It is difficult to quantify the cost (emotional, physical, financial, etc.) of widespread sexual abuse in our society, experienced by an estimated 1 in 3 women and 1 in 6 men, as mentioned earlier. We can speak more clearly to impacts on individuals.

In order to describe some ways that sexual abuse affects victims, we will tell a fictitious story about a sexual offense. The template we will use to describe this scenario is called a "sexual offense cycle." It comes from *Cognitive Behavioral Therapy*.[3] Originally, it was used for people struggling with addictions to explain how thoughts, feelings, and behaviors work together to create unhealthy patterns, and later, addictions. Since that time, therapists and others have recognized the value of using it with sex offenders to help them understand habits that lead to offending. Although this cycle does not explain all sexual abuse and perhaps is too simplistic, it allows us to understand that sexual offending is a choice. The cycle can even explain sexual offending where an offender is diagnosed with a psychiatric disorder like pedophilia, which indicates a sexual attraction toward certain ages of children. Really, all human choice reflects thoughts, feelings, behaviors, and experiences. A sexual abuse cycle simply connects these to each other.

1.  **Life stresses:** This model begins with life stress. Most, if not all, people will experience stress at some point in adulthood, occasioned by family, relational, and/or financial issues. The challenge is how to cope with it.

    Human beings typically respond to stress (a) internally—as the brain processes the experience based on how it has developed—and (b) externally—through behaviors. A history of early sexualization and/or childhood trauma—neglect, abuse, etc.—is often (but not always) a part of a sex offender's development. Trauma alters the stress responses of the brain. That is, the human brain can be damaged by it, so much so that stress that should be experienced as normal is experienced as a matter of life or death, fight or flight. Stress often precipitates or triggers violence when the chosen means of coping with it are unhealthy.

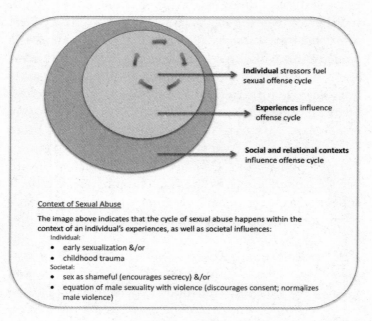

Individual stressors fuel sexual offense cycle

Experiences influence offense cycle

Social and relational contexts influence offense cycle

<u>Context of Sexual Abuse</u>

The image above indicates that the cycle of sexual abuse happens within the context of an individual's experiences, as well as societal influences:

Individual:
- early sexualization &/or
- childhood trauma

Societal:
- sex as shameful (encourages secrecy) &/or
- equation of male sexuality with violence (discourages consent; normalizes male violence)

*For our example, let us imagine that a man in this cycle is experiencing significant marital stress with his victim's mother. This triggers in him a fear of abandonment. Along with fear comes embarrassment at his own failure to maintain healthy relationships. He decides to try to "tough it out" and not tell anyone about his relational stress. Instead, he begins to cope in unhealthy ways.*

2.  **Preparation:** Most of the preparatory work for sexual offending is a combination of two factors: first, unhealthy coping combined with the second, conscious or unconscious grooming of a potential victim. The first is about using unhelpful ways to deal with difficult emotions. The second, grooming, means establishing a relationship of trust

with a victim and thus creating an opportunity for sexual offending. One effect of trauma, because of a damaged stress response, is that traumatized people often have a hard time being in healthy relationships with others. Psychologists often call this *disorganized attachment*—i.e., difficulty bonding with others. Those who sexually offend are often emotionally immature, more comfortable relating to children than adults.

*The man in our story experiences the marital stress as an uncontrollable hardship. He feels overwhelmed by it. He feels embarrassed that he is failing at something that he views as important. He blames his partner for what he perceives as her unwillingness to reciprocate effort in the relationship. He fails to recognize or acknowledge his own responsibility. He is angry and confused. He is nostalgic for how he imagines the relationship was in the past. In order to deal with these intense feelings, he withdraws. He does not talk to anyone about his unhappiness. He thinks people will not understand. During this time, he starts to fantasize more and increasingly uses pornography and masturbation as a way to soothe himself. Alcohol becomes his friend. Not previously a heavy drinker, he consumes beer at every opportunity.*

*As the adult relationship gets worse, the man is more often alone with his stepdaughter. His partner works in the evening, so the man becomes the primary caregiver. After dinners, the man and child often watch television together. For many weeks, the only physical contact is appropriate cuddling between a stepfather and stepdaughter. However, without acknowledging it, this contact is starting to fill an emotional need for the man, and he begins to sexualize it—that is, he thinks*

*about touching her inappropriately. Initially, he is able
to shake off these thoughts, but the angrier he gets at his
partner, the more he loses his grip on reality. The more
he drinks, the less he is able to think clearly about his
responsibility as an adult to a child. The more he withdraws, the more he feels like a "loser" and a "good for
nothing" person. The more time he spends with the child
in this unhealthy state, the more he chooses to think that
only she "understands him," that she "wants to be with
him." The child is oblivious to his inner turmoil. She is
simply grateful for his attention and affection.*

3. **Sexual offending:** In order to sexually offend,
   people have to give themselves permission. Sexual
   abuse is a choice offenders make. Choices might be
   influenced by previous traumatic experiences, but
   even those with experiences of sexual victimization do not usually go on to perpetrate it. Where
   does this permission come from? Some permission
   is social. Masculinity is socially constructed in a
   way that gives men permission to act violently,
   especially with regard to sex.

   - The majority of perpetrators of sexual offenses
     are male: research studies show that the most
     consistent predictor of sexual victimization is
     being exposed to a sexually aggressive man.[4]
   - 90% of perpetrators are known to victims,
     most often a family member or friend.[5]

   The term "rape culture" is used to describe how
   men are socialized to sexually take what they
   want, when they want it, regardless of consent.
   When men use their power over others, sexually

abusing women, girls, boys, and other men, society often sides with the offender, blaming the victim. Common ways that people blame victims:

- "She must have done something to provoke it."
- "If she wasn't wearing that short skirt, he wouldn't have sexually assaulted her."
- "He was always causing problems and making up stories."
- "She didn't say 'no.'"
- "If he didn't like it, why did he keep spending time with the offender?"

Rape culture, rooted in patriarchy and a toxic expression of masculinity, has a profoundly negative impact on all women and girls. Rape culture trickles into many social institutions, including the family, faith communities, and schools. Colleges and universities, for example, are at the center of these statistics:

- Approximately 25% of women will experience completed or attempted rape over the course of a college career.[6]
- As many as 13% of women attending college are victimized by stalking.[7]
- Multiple studies across different decades have consistently found that 35% of college men indicated they would likely perpetrate rape if they knew they would not get caught.[8]

Given a social context that gives a man permission to be sexually violent, there is also much about an individual's patterns of behavior that can influence whether he gives himself permission to do so. If he blames others for his problems, if he withdraws, if he uses maladaptive coping mechanisms (drugs, alcohol, pornography) to deal with difficult emotions, and/or if he sexualizes relationships with children, he is choosing an unhealthy pattern of behavior. Each of these elements follows a process of, first, dehumanizing himself by disconnecting from others and his responsibility for his choices and, second, dehumanizing or objectifying a potential victim. All of it, individual and context, adds up to permission to violate.

*The man convinces himself that the child appreciates his sexual advances. Over the past few days, he has moved his hand closer to her genitals, confusing her fear, her powerlessness to stop his actions, as a twisted form of consent. Finally, he betrays her trust, betrays his role as a caregiver, betrays his role as a partner, betrays his community, and sexually abuses his stepdaughter. He overpowers her, he hurts the child and, by extension, many who love and care for both of them.*

4. **Shame:** *Later that night, at first, he is absolutely disgusted with himself. How could he have done something like this? He's "sick, a monster!" Quickly though, he buries his shame, recognizing that if anyone finds out, he'll go to jail. He told her not to tell anyone what he did. That it was their special secret, a part of a special relationship. Later, he knows he can make other threats like "the police will take me away if anyone finds out, and you won't have a dad." And "doesn't it feel good, anyway?"*

Offenders often feel shame and guilt after perpetrating sexual abuse. However, minimizing, rationalizing, or justifying harm easily buries these emotions. Secrecy by threat is a way that sexual abuse carries on. Sexual abuse itself often renders victims silent, yet offenders often use further threatening tactics to coerce their continued silence.

5. **Justification:** One way to not take responsibility for harmful behavior is to justify it.

    *So, he does: "it wasn't really that bad" (minimize); "she seemed to invite and like it"(justify); "it's better for all of us if no one finds out" (rationalize); "my brother did the same thing to me when I was little and I got over it" (minimize and rationalize); "it's important for her to understand how her body works" (justify).* As the justifications build one upon the other, it becomes easier for the offender to offend again.

# Impacts of sexual abuse

Typically, though not always, sexual abuse is experienced as traumatic. Trauma is an experience that overwhelms a person's ability to cope. In the moment, the person believes that life is over. The survival mechanisms of fight (attack back), flight (run away), or freeze (helpless to do either fight or flight) are triggered. Often, when the survival mechanism is triggered, it remains on until the person has opportunity to heal, which is why trauma survivors often feel controlled by past abuses. If stuck in fight mode, a survivor might remain aggressive in many situations, even those that do not call for an attack. If stuck in flight mode, a survivor might withdraw from relationships. If frozen, a person might be numb, consistently feeling helpless. Possibly, a victim might swing between all three of these reactions. Regardless, the stress response of the survivor is damaged by trauma.

All efforts are made to avoid the trauma's resurfacing, which is why many survivors cope using alcohol, drugs, sex, and/or violence. However, in spite of these coping strategies, reminders of trauma flood the survivor's senses: certain sights, sounds, smells, tastes, and touches return the survivor to the time of the trauma. The violence reappears while awake through the senses and often in nightmares while they sleep. Perpetually stuck, sexual abuse victims often develop mental health challenges like post-traumatic stress disorder (PTSD), depression, anxiety, and dissociative identity disorder.

Sexual abuse is often regarded by victims as shameful. Survivors often blame themselves, even if offenders and

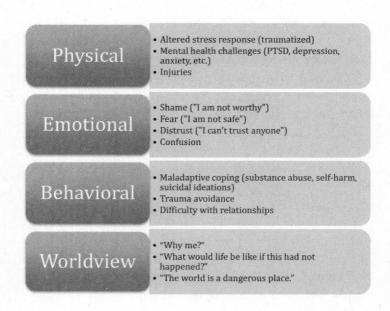

**Physical**
- Altered stress response (traumatized)
- Mental health challenges (PTSD, depression, anxiety, etc.)
- Injuries

**Emotional**
- Shame ("I am not worthy")
- Fear ("I am not safe")
- Distrust ("I can't trust anyone")
- Confusion

**Behavioral**
- Maladaptive coping (substance abuse, self-harm, suicidal ideations)
- Trauma avoidance
- Difficulty with relationships

**Worldview**
- "Why me?"
- "What would life be like if this had not happened?"
- "The world is a dangerous place."

society do not. I (Judah) often use the work of researcher Brene Brown to explain shame: she says that it makes us feel that our core identity is "bad," or unworthy of human connection.[9] Furthermore, as the majority of sexual abuse is perpetrated by someone known to the victim, survivors find it hard to trust others afterward. Why should they? If those who are supposed to love and care for victims can also cause them the most hurt, it is hard to have a positive outlook on relationships, or the world. Trauma creates relational challenges as victims consistently feel unsafe.

In this chapter, we have defined the terms "sexual abuse," "victim," and "offender." We have used a sexual offense cycle to explain how sexual offending is a choice, embedded within an offender's thoughts, feelings, behaviors, experiences, and context. We have explained some of the traumatic consequences of sexual abuse on victims. In the next chapter, we will explain restorative justice as a framework to set up later chapters that highlight how it can be used to help victims, offenders, and communities find hope through trauma.

3

# Restorative Justice

Restorative Justice is first and foremost a framework for addressing and preventing harm. As a philosophy, it is about moving beyond punishment to recognizing that, when rule-breaking events like crimes happen, individuals and relationships are most directly affected. Rules and laws are still important, and the desire for vindication that we feel when treated unjustly must be acknowledged. However, healing human beings, relationships, and communities are the primary focus of restorative justice.

When Mark Yantzi, a young probation officer in Kitchener, Ontario (Canada), had a group of youths meet the victims of their vandalism spree in 1974, it sparked some fundamental questions about justice practices and the needs of people affected by crime. In the early 1980s, Howard Zehr began to articulate an ethos undergirding this approach. In his foundational work *Changing Lenses* and later in *The Little Book of Restorative Justice,* Zehr suggests that a restorative justice orientation asks questions such as these after crime or harm:

1. Who has been hurt?
2. What do they need?
3. Whose obligations are they?
4. What are the root causes?
5. How do we engage relevant stakeholders in addressing these needs and obligations?
6. What needs to be done to make things as right as possible, including addressing root causes?

Since that time, restorative justice has been implemented in many other spheres beyond criminal justice, including schools, child protection, and the workplace. As a practice, it often involves some type of dialogue or encounter between people who have been hurt, those who have caused harm, and community members. However, some programs focus solely on offenders, some exclusively on victims, and others more on community development and prevention. Restorative practices are best seen as a continuum of approaches, implementing a restorative justice framework in full or in part.

Zehr and other modern restorative justice experts acknowledge that the roots of restorative justice extend much deeper than the 1970s-era experiments. In fact, many indigenous and religious traditions practice forms of restorative justice. In chapter 7, when we discuss the Hollow Water case, we will see some strong connections between one indigenous form of justice and the way restorative justice is articulated in this book. The modern restorative justice movement owes much to indigenous communities around the world for maintaining and encouraging justice practices that are more about healing than punishment, that offer a more holistic, community-rooted vision for a healthy way of life.

## Justice as meeting needs

Essentially, restorative justice orients justice responses around what people *need* after crime or harm. Justice, then, is best understood as meeting the needs of victims, offenders, and communities toward the purpose of healing. Using the lens of restorative justice, researchers and practitioners articulate a common set of needs for each of these groups. Of course, not every need is relevant to every person. It is important to listen—not to impose one's vision of justice on others.

# What do victims of sexual abuse need?

| Need | Description |
|---|---|
| Safety & care | • Abuse has to stop before people can heal.<br>• Physical and emotional safety should be of primary importance.<br>• Safe, supportive relationships need to be established. Caregivers must be consistent, authentic, and patient, allowing victims an opportunity to learn to trust again.<br>• In certain contexts, safety means separating an offender from a victim. |
| Believed, absolved, & vindicated | • People, especially children, rarely lie about being sexually abused. It is important to say, "I believe you."<br>• Victims often blame themselves, however unfounded this is. Saying "It was not your fault" is needed.<br>• "What happened to you was wrong" acknowledges that sexual abuse is harmful and not okay. |
| Voice & empowerment | • Victims' voices need to be heard. Safe space must be provided for their stories.<br>• Sexual abuse is disempowering, beyond the control of victims. Helping victims generate choices moves them toward healing and regaining control of their lives. |
| Grieving & expression | • Victims need safe space to mourn their pains.<br>• Victims need exploration of identity, including impact on their sexual being.<br>• Expression of the impacts—sometimes directly to the offender—is often important. |
| Support & education | • Victims need access to supports that foster resiliency. It is important to recognize that restorative justice is only one layer of support; others are likely necessary for victims to move toward healing.<br>• Education helps people understand that PTSD is a normal response to an abnormal event. Often when people experience the trauma of sexual abuse, they feel like they are "losing their mind" or "crazy."<br>• Gaining clarity—for example, if a male victim gets an erection or ejaculates or a female victim experiences an orgasm while being abused, it does not mean he or she "liked" or "wanted" it. |

| Need | Description |
|---|---|
| Information & options | • Options: What support is available? How can it help? Answers to questions (sometimes sought from the offender). What is the offender doing to make sure it never happens again? |
| Accountability | • Permission to make mistakes, coupled with support toward healing, is crucial. At the same time, victims may need to be asked about unhealthy coping strategies or choices: "How is that working for you?" |

# What are the needs of people who have offended sexually?

Punishment alone will not make communities safer. US Attorney General Eric Holder said this in reference to drug crimes, but it also applies to sexual offenses: "We can't incarcerate our way to being a safer nation."[10] Regardless of our beliefs about what should happen to sex offenders—some might say the death penalty, others "put them on an island"—most will be released from prison and resume living within society. This means that we must find a meaningful way to work with them. The challenge of a restorative justice orientation with people who have offended sexually is balancing accountability with support.

- What does a person who has offended sexually need to do in order to take responsibility? (accountability)
- What does a person who has offended sexually need in order to heal? (support)

## *Accountability*

Taking responsibility means naming wrongdoing ("I did XYZ"), acknowledging harm done ("As a result, here's how people are hurting . . ."), seeking to make reparations ("I will make sure it never happens again by . . ."), and making things as right as possible ("I will seek to make reparations by . . ."). Accountability is a process, often a slowly explored pathway from denial and justification.

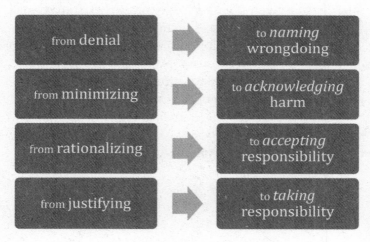

How is this best accomplished? Restorative justice processes are invitational; that is, they hold a person accountable within a context of support. The hope is that the more we treat a person with kindness, the more he/she will learn to do the same. It is not naïve, nor is it minimizing or even denying wrongdoing. It is about treating an offender with dignity and respect, so he/she can face harmful choices by learning to understand offense cycles, and implementing future safety plans. Restorative justice is practical, based in reality. Sex offenders often need regular supervision, to be monitored more closely than others. Restorative justice demands clear boundaries, behavioral expectations, and the difficult work of taking responsibility. The priority is always safety.

## Support

To commit a sexual offense takes a certain amount of brokenness. Restorative justice assumes that this type of violence is not natural. Is it a sickness? Is it an error in thinking or judgment? Is it a re-enactment of a person's own childhood traumas? It is important that sex offenders be given safe space to explore these questions. It is helpful for restorative justice programs to adopt a trauma-informed lens for support. When people have been traumatized, they often relate to others differently. Relationships can become characterized by conflict and violence because of distrust and underdeveloped or compromised emotional maturity. Many sex offenders have histories of childhood trauma. Support provides a context for healing as well as accountability.

## Incapacitation

Restorative justice is not foolproof. Many sex offenders are not up to the challenge of taking responsibility and are therefore dangerous to themselves and others. The criminal justice system can incapacitate. Restorative justice cannot. However, an ethos of restorative justice can still be maintained. For example, Barb Toews talks about using it in prison contexts in her *Little Book of Restorative Justice for People in Prison*. Restorative justice is concerned with humane incapacitation. Does prison damage the psyche of an inmate and make him or her more dangerous, or does it incapacitate in a way that promotes rehabilitation and interconnection? As a society, we have to take responsibility for our interventions: do they encourage accountability or simply do more harm?

## Belief

At its core, restorative justice believes in a person's ability to change. As much as people are capable of tremendous harm, with the right support, they also have the capacity for transformation. Often offenders and others around them have given up. A restorative justice approach believes in the possibility of nonviolent relationships. Change requires safe space for offenders to be vulnerable, to understand themselves as well as the harm they have committed. Brene Brown tells us that vulnerability moves people away from shame, toward empathy.[11] The more empathy a person feels, the less likely it is that he or she will harm others in the future.

## Partnership

Sex offenders need communities and professionals to communicate with each other. Sexual offending happens in secrecy, but holding offenders accountable cannot. It is important for restorative justice practitioners to regularly talk to justice professionals and therapists. The tasks of accountability, support, incapacitation, and belief cannot be done in isolation without multiple stakeholders.

# What do communities need?

Communities are also victims of sexual abuse. Sometimes it is a family, traumatized by the actions of one of their own. Sometimes it may be a faith community, horrified by revelations of sexual abuse by a trusted leader. Other times it is a college campus fearful that sexual assaults might be repeated. Communities have needs as victims: for safety, information, voice, empowerment, and education. Communities also have a responsibility. What can they do to eliminate root causes of sexual abuse? How can communities respond to sexual abuse in a way that future harms are prevented? How can they best support victims and offenders while holding offenders appropriately accountable? Justice is a community issue.

Once we understand justice as meeting the needs of people who have been hurt and those who have caused harm, we can articulate some principles of a restorative justice approach to sexual abuse:

**Key principles of restorative justice for responding to sexual abuse.**

1. Believe victims.
2. Establish physical and emotional safety for victims.
3. Create opportunities for victims to heal: empowerment through choice.
4. Offenders are to be held accountable within a context of support. Where unaccountable, separation and incapacitation is an option.
5. Offenders are encouraged to acknowledge wrongdoing, identify their sexual offense cycle, and work toward empathy (understanding the impacts of sexual abuse) and change.
6. The needs of community members as victims are identified and addressed.

7. The obligations of community members to change contexts that support sexual offending are identified and addressed.

## Key principles of restorative justice for preventing sexual abuse.

1. Restorative justice undermines the secrecy of sexual abuse by talking about it.
2. Building supportive, accountable, healthy relationships with victims, offenders, and communities contributes to no further harm.
3. Communities need ownership of conflict and violence resolution.

## Key principles for restorative justice practitioners.

1. A collaborative approach with other professionals is most effective. These can include criminal justice and therapeutic professionals.
2. Practitioners are better equipped when they can articulate why sexual offending is linked to patriarchy, a system that perpetuates gender-based violence. Men are more likely to be perpetrators.
3. Practitioners are better equipped when they are trauma-informed.
4. Practitioners are better equipped when they understand sexual offending as a cycle.
5. Restorative justice programs are not always the best or most complete option for meeting justice needs. Practitioners need to know their limitations.

In short, restorative justice is a framework for addressing and preventing harm. From this perspective, justice first meets the needs of victims and, second, holds offenders accountable within a context of support. The wider community must also be considered. In the next few chapters, we will provide case stories, followed by observations, to explain how restorative justice might be applied more specifically to each of these stakeholders.

# 4

# Victims

## *A case study*

---

The following story, a composite of common situations, brings together a number of themes related to experiences of sexual victimization.

*Brenda was sexually abused by her stepfather Tony. It started when she was eight, not long after he moved in with her family. Mostly the sexual abuse happened while her mom was out at work, but it also happened when everyone else in the house was sleeping. From the outside looking in, no one would have guessed that Tony was a sexual offender. He was soft-spoken, gentle, and did a lot for his community. In fact, he also did a lot for Brenda, helping her with her homework and coaching her baseball team.*

*Brenda actually tried when she was ten to tell her mom, but her mom became angry—refused to believe her—and told her to never again say such horrible things. Brenda's world was turned upside down, especially after the attempted disclosure. She withdrew at school. She started self-harming, stabbing her legs with pens until she drew blood. Teachers thought she was a problem. Her friends' parents thought she was a problem. She thought she was a problem.*

*When Brenda was thirteen, her stepfather raped her, and she became pregnant. An abortion was secretly arranged—the medical staff were told she had been promiscuous with some older boys. By fifteen, Brenda was finally able to stop the sexual abuse—but only after running away from home. By this time, she was heavily into drugs, had been diagnosed with bipolar disorder, and had attempted suicide on a number of occasions. By her early twenties, she had been in a series of abusive relationships with men. Finally, with the help of a friend who believed her stories of victimization and gave her support, Brenda began to address what had happened to her and to heal.*

This story is a fairly common example of the experiences of sexual abuse survivors: manipulation, betrayal of trust, and abuse by a family member, leading to a host of problems, and often damaging other close relationships. The patterns are similar to those the cycle described previously. This chapter explores some restorative justice options for response and compares them to therapeutic and legal ones. Finishing with examples of programs, the chapter highlights the need for holistic, resourced responses to victimization.

## Therapy, criminal justice, and restorative justice

Sexual assault support centers have been in the trenches for decades, offering support to female survivors of sexual abuse and more recently to males as well. The support they offer, usually on a shoe-string budget, is remarkable. Here, survivors are able to access individual as well as group counseling. Typically, sexual assault support centers also help survivors create safety plans and offer court accompaniment. Staff also does public education work to combat societal myths that lead survivors to maintain silence and to raise awareness about sexual abuse. Other professionals and organizations, such as psychologists and counseling agencies, also offer therapeutic services.

Therapy can meet many needs of victims. In the scenario above, Brenda would likely benefit from counseling— someone to talk to. In the words of trauma specialist Judith Herman, it is important to remember, mourn and reconnect.[12] Naming and describing abuse, putting it into narrative form, is often helpful. The opportunity to emerge from emotional and physical harm—which can be tremendously isolating—and to connect with others in healthy relationships is important. Human beings are social by nature; we need others to be fully human. Often, survivors of sexual abuse need space to wonder how their lives might have been different if they had not been abused. Brenda needs space to grieve, to figure out how she is going to choose to understand and articulate this part of her life.

Criminal justice responses are also available to victims. Brenda might choose to report the abuse to police. She might be hoping that the courts validate her traumatic experiences. When a judge finds an offender guilty and sentences him or her, this can provide one avenue for a victim's pain to be acknowledged. However, western criminal justice systems have notoriously low arrest and conviction rates, often less than 5%. Legal justice is about fact-finding, an attempt to prove the truth.

An offender is innocent until proven guilty. I (Judah) heard one survivor of sexual abuse describe the victim experience in court as *"lying until proven truthful."*

When the criminal justice system gets involved, victims often lose control of their case. Brenda may have very little say in what happens after she reports the crime. If the offender pleads not-guilty, the victim will likely be cross-examined by the offender's attorney in an attempt to discredit the victim's story.

Brenda might also go to the police because she is worried about the offender hurting others. She wants to make sure she stops him. Although it is not their responsibility, survivors often carry this weight. At its core, they want to make sure that what happened to them never happens to anyone else. When the only perceived mechanism for accomplishing this is prison, survivors will turn to the criminal justice system, even where they feel ambivalent toward an offender (i.e., they might not need or want him to suffer as they did). Although conviction rates are low and victims often speak about re-victimization through the process (i.e., cross-examination), some do experience vindication through criminal justice.

## Restorative justice and victims of sexual abuse

Restorative justice practitioners have envisioned a number of programmatic options for supporting survivors. Some are encounter-based: opportunities, where appropriate, for facilitated dialogues between victims, offenders, and community members. Some are support-based: focused specifically on meeting the needs of victims for healing. Regardless of the program, it is important to remember that restorative justice is primarily a framework. The principles from the previous chapter, along with understanding common victim needs, can function like a guide for working with victims.

## Needs that restorative justice dialogue can address

Restorative justice dialogue in the form of a facilitated face-to-face meeting is one option. Sometimes victims want an offender to understand how much their lives have been affected. Other times, they have questions or want to find out whether the offender is remorseful. Restorative justice dialogue can fill a gap in therapy and criminal justice by providing opportunities (where appropriate) for facilitated dialogue between victims and offenders.

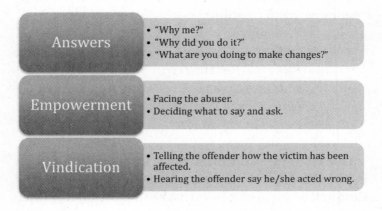

| Answers | • "Why me?" <br> • "Why did you do it?" <br> • "What are you doing to make changes?" |
| Empowerment | • Facing the abuser. <br> • Deciding what to say and ask. |
| Vindication | • Telling the offender how the victim has been affected. <br> • Hearing the offender say he/she acted wrong. |

Going through a restorative justice dialogue can be empowering for victims. However, it takes tremendous courage to directly face a person who has caused so much hurt. Consequently, there is much preparatory work for restorative justice facilitators to do with both victim and offender (and support persons) to make sure a dialogue is going to be positive. Not only should facilitators have background knowledge of trauma, they ought not to function in isolation. At a minimum, they should be accountable to other staff, if not working in collaboration with other service providers, like therapists and criminal justice professionals. For this reason, many restorative justice dialogue programs use at least two co-facilitators. Lorraine Stutzman Amstutz describes the lengthy preparatory work involved for a dialogue process in her *Little Book of Victim Offender Conferencing: Bringing Victims and Offenders Together in Dialogue*. Some considerations are safety, supports, mental health issues, suicidal ideations, addictions, culture, goals for participating, hopes for what the dialogue will accomplish, etc.

Other *Little Books* that explore encounter-based restorative justice options:

- *The Little Book of Family Group Conferences* by Allan MacRae and Howard Zehr
- *The Little Book of Circle Processes* by Kay Pranis
- *The Little Book of Restorative Justice for Colleges and Universities* by David Karp

One example of a victim-offender dialogue program is the Restorative Opportunities program of the Restorative Justice Division at the Correctional Service Canada. This program provides opportunities for safe, facilitated contact between victims and federally sentenced offenders (those with a sentence of greater than two years). Contact can include an exchange of letters, shuttle mediation, video, or face-to-face conversation. All contact is facilitated by highly trained mediators who perform lengthy assessment work to screen for suitability.

**Restorative Opportunities, Correctional Service Canada:**

*Program Description*: It "offers people who have been harmed by a crime, either directly or indirectly, a chance to communicate with the offender who caused harm. [It] is a post-sentence program in which participation is voluntary for everyone concerned. The program explores opportunities to use various victim-offender mediation models that best suit the needs of participants, as defined by the participants, with the help of a professional mediator. . . . [V]ictims can tell their story, explain to the offender the crime's physical, emotional and financial impact on their lives, explore unanswered questions about the crime and the offender, and participate directly in developing options to try to address the harms caused, where possible."

**From: www.csc-scc.gc.ca/restorative-justice/003005-1000-eng.shtml**

Restorative justice dialogue has some limitations. First, it requires an offender to be caught, which is not often the case in situations of sexual abuse. Second, restorative justice programs require offenders to take some measure of responsibility for their behavior. Not all offenders are willing to be accountable. Third, the restorative justice approach is limited at best. Restorative justice dialogue is not always appropriate or possible.

## Support-based restorative justice with victims of sexual abuse

In light of this, some restorative justice programs focus solely on offering supports to survivors. An example of this is the peer support program at Community Justice Initiatives (CJI) in Kitchener, Canada.

---

**Survivor Program, Community Justice Initiatives (CJI) of Waterloo Region:**

*Program Description*: Premised on principles of restorative justice, CJI offers peer support and education groups for survivors of sexual abuse. Topics from the educational component include self-care, identifying emotions, body image, and building healthy relationships. Support groups, facilitated by trained community volunteers, offer space where survivors can care for each other, reduce isolation, and share challenges of survivorship.

**From: www.cjiwr.com/survivor-support.htm**

---

## Research on restorative justice and sexual abuse victims

Often restorative justice programs have been reluctant—for reasons of safety, re-victimization, etc.—to take on cases of sexual abuse and/or domestic violence. With a need to expand options for victims and to meet their requests for safe alternatives to therapy and criminal justice, some programs carefully offer supports or programs in this area. Research on this topic is preliminary, but a few research articles identify restorative justice as a promising practice.

- One study by Kathleen Daly tracked 400 sexual assault cases perpetrated by youth in Australia and compared outcomes of those that used a court process versus those that used a restorative justice conference.[13] The study concluded that victims were less prone to re-victimization by a restorative justice process as offenders were admitting guilt, taking responsibility, and being moved in the direction of treatment. Offenders who went through the conference were also less likely to re-offend.
- A study by Clare McGlynn, Nicole Westmarland, and Nikki Godden used a case study of dialogue between a survivor of sexual abuse and her offender to explore opportunities for restorative justice to meet victim needs.[14] The authors suggest some possibility for such dialogue because, with appropriate preparation, victims are able to speak in ways that they define, ask questions that are important to them, have their experience honored, and take back some personal power.
- Studies on victim satisfaction after participating in restorative justice processes highlight that restorative justice typically outperforms the traditional criminal justice system. A study by Tinneke Van Camp and Jo-Anne Wemmers found that victims are often satisfied because they view restorative justice as procedurally just: their voices are heard,

they have input on outcomes, and mediators are trustworthy and impartial.[15]

Research affirms the need for interventions that:

1. honor what victims have been through;
2. empower victims to control how they will name their experiences;
3. and promote offender accountability.

Research also identifies concerns that should be considered by restorative justice:

1. Is victim safety appropriately considered (including power imbalances)?
2. Is restorative justice at risk of making sexual violence a less than legal/criminal issue by diverting it back to the community (i.e., re-privatizing gender-based violence)?

In summary, a restorative justice framework expands the options available for victims of sexual abuse to experience some form of justice. Furthermore, their needs are prioritized. In practice, restorative justice programs have typically offered dialogue processes. This is largely a result of victims' requests for support to talk with others about their traumatic experiences, sometimes including with offenders. In the next chapter, we shift to talking about people who have offended sexually.

5

# Offenders

## *A case study*

---

*M*ichael was adamant, when arrested in a sting operation for soliciting sex with a minor, that this was the first time he had been involved in this kind of activity. While acknowledging that he had upon occasion looked at child pornography on the Internet, he said he had never acted on any urges until now. Five years and a three-year prison term later, Michael believes that his actions were a result of abuse he suffered as a child at the hands of a family member. He acknowledges, however, that this is not an excuse for the abuse he committed himself. He admits to the bad choices that he made and recognizes that he'll pay for those choices the rest *of his life as a registered sex offender. He knows that our society views him as, what he terms, a "modern-day leper." He will need to earn the trust of those who have chosen to be involved in his life and to keep him accountable.*

According to the National Center for Missing and Exploited Children, there are 747,000 registered sex offenders in the US and 16,295 registered sex offenders in Canada.[16] Many of those sex offenders will be returning to our communities following their incarceration. Unfortunately, not many will have a group of supporters to walk with them on a daily basis. Given the repulsion our society has toward those who have committed sex crimes, offenders are intentionally isolated by laws intended to decrease the risk to our communities. Some sex offenders are prohibited by law from living within close proximity to schools, daycare centers, parks, or playgrounds. Some cities expand this list to swimming pools, bus stops, libraries, and other places where children are likely to be present. There is some merit in restricting access to children against people who have offended sexually against children; however, the unintended consequences of these laws are that they may exacerbate stressors for those struggling to find a way to live successfully in our communities. By adding to already present isolation and shame, society might be contributing to known factors that influence re-offending.

Judge Dennis Challeen has summarized what we do to offenders like this:

We want them to have self-worth . . .
 *So we destroy their self-worth.*
We want them to be responsible . . . .
 *So we take away all responsibilities.*

We want them to be part of our community . . .
>*So we isolate them from our community.*

We want them to be positive and constructive . . .
>*So we degrade them and make them useless.*

We want them to be trustworthy . . .
>*So we put them where there is no trust.*

We want them to be nonviolent . . .
>*So we put them where there is violence all around them.*

We want them to be kind and loving people . . .
>*So we subject them to hatred and cruelty.*

We want them to quit being the tough guy . . .
>*So we put them where the tough guy is respected.*

We want them to quit hanging around losers . . .
>*So we put all the losers in the state under one roof.*

We want them to quit exploiting us . . .
>*So we put them where they exploit each other.*

We want them to take control of their lives, own their problems, and quit being a parasite . . .
>*So we make them totally dependent on us.*[17]

## Where is the hope?

Hope is defined as the feeling that what is wanted can be had or that events *will* turn out for the best. We know that having hope gives us reason to move forward in healthy ways, to be able to take responsibility for our behavior, to engage in pro-social ways with our environment. When people are remembered for the worst thing they ever did rather than the good they have contributed, hope is difficult to maintain. To illustrate, Dr. Martin Seligman, of the Berkley Swim Team, conducted a study that looks at swimmers who were scored as either "optimists" or "pessimists." He timed the swimmers on their first heat; after, he told them each a time that was slower than their real time. Then, on the second heat, one group (the optimists) swam faster, and the second group (the pessimists) swam slower.[18] How do we create optimism in those we continue to isolate and degrade? If we believe that our goal is to have "no more victims," then we need to not only hope for change in behavior but also create pathways to increase hope for those who have offended.

Given the difficulties sex offenders face while reintegrating into our communities and the public's concerns, how do we work in ways that include accountability and support for offenders and their loved ones?

## Offender reintegration

Controversy surrounds treatment for sex offenders. The challenge, many would agree, is that one size does not fit all. Sex offenders are not a homogenous group, and treatment needs to be tailored to specific needs that address the reasons for each person's harmful behavior. Not all sex offenders are at high risk for re-offending. Advances are being made to more accurately identify factors that increase the likelihood of re-offending so that precautions and treatment are more effective.

As we consider the values and principles of restorative justice, we know that important forms of treatment are those that strive for a holistic balance of the emotional, mental, physical, social, and spiritual parts of a person. Acknowledging that these are interconnected, we must also focus on the strengths of an individual—not only on the negative aspects of a person's behavior.

> When we feel connected and know that we matter, we are better able to live up to our full potential.

In Palm Beach County, Florida, *Miracle Village* was established by the late pastor Dick Witherow when he saw the difficulty sex offenders had in trying to find a place to live. About 200 people live in this village, which is nearly two miles from the nearest town. Over 100 are registered sex offenders. They are just as concerned about safety and prevention as any other community. While it is a Christian community, non-Christians are welcome in the village. There are Bible and anger management classes, and most of the sex offenders attend treatment programs. They are monitored weekly by a detective from the Sexual Predator and Offender Tracking Unit as they work at living in community.[19]

In 1994, Mennonite Central Committee Canada developed *Circles of Support and Accountability (COSA)* to assist communities in responding to the release of high-risk sex offenders. These offenders were returning to communities with no additional supports, accountability requirements, or supervision by Correctional Services Canada (CSC). CSC Chaplaincy supports this program and provides four to seven volunteers who commit to meeting and regularly supporting a sex offender. The COSA Mission Statement is "to substantially reduce the risk of future sexual victimization of community members by assisting and supporting released individuals in their task of integrating with the community and leading responsible, productive, and accountable lives."[20]

COSA core values in seeking to live out that mission include:

- We affirm that the community bears a responsibility for the safe restoration and healing of victims as well as the safe re-entry of released sex offenders into the community.
- We believe in a loving and reconciling Creator who calls us to be agents in the work of healing. (COSA programs are often faith-based.)
- We acknowledge the ongoing pain and need for healing among victims and survivors of sexual abuse and sexual assault.
- We seek to "recreate community" with former offenders in responsible, safe, healthy, and life-giving ways.
- We accept the challenge of radical hospitality, sharing our lives with one another in community and taking risks in the service of love.[21]

Principles of restorative justice undergird the COSA work. Volunteers commit to meeting at least once a week with a "core member" (a term that identifies the offender in a less stigmatizing way), and may meet daily if necessary (especially upon initial release of the core member from prison). In the US, one COSA program was developed by a Mennonite pastor, Clare Ann Ruth-Heffelbower, who won a $290,000 grant for it from the California Dept. of Corrections and Rehabilitation. She says that "COSA's success is simplicity. It follows two guiding principles: no more victims, and no one is disposable."[22] Not that simplicity is easy, but understanding that when a community takes responsibility for its members, rather than relegating that task to an "other," the investment in people's lives makes it a safer, healthier place to live.

# Research on circles of support and accountability

There is a growing body of research on the effectiveness of COSA. Studies indicate that community members feel safer knowing that high-risk sex offenders have adequate supports and connections. COSA is helping to put communities at ease and is also dramatically reducing re-offending.

- One longitudinal study, conducted by Robin Wilson, Janine Pechaca, and Michelle Prinzo, found that sex offenders who participated in COSA were 70% less likely to re-offend than a control group (i.e., similar offenders not involved in COSA).[23]
- People consistently ask, "Why does it work so well?" Mechtild Hoing, Stefan Bogaerts, Bas Vogelvang, and other researchers have responded by highlighting its core principle of inclusion.[24] The more people feel included, the more likely they are to live in pro-social ways.

Thus, research continues to reinforce one of the premises of restorative justice that accountability happens best within a context of support. None of this minimizes the importance or validity of the harm already done to victims. It simply means that effective interventions, in the words of researcher Alan Jenkins who has worked for many decades with offenders, must provide "safe passage" for people who have caused harm.[25] Furthermore, fostering hope also includes offenders fulfilling their obligations to be accountable to victims and communities.

## Accountability

A restorative justice framework promotes taking responsibility beyond simply "doing time." Some offenders should be incarcerated. However, if punishment is the only tool for dealing with people who offend sexually, then accountability is diminished.

The following are some essential characteristics of accountability:

- Restorative justice encourages **empathy**. An offender should work toward understanding how their actions have harmed people and relationships.
- Restorative justice is not satisfied with the status quo: offenders should be taking steps toward **change**. Why do they perpetrate sexual abuse? What do they need to change about their thoughts, behaviors, and circumstances?
- Restorative justice values **community safety**. Some offenders are more concerned with how getting caught has affected their lives rather than with remorse. The COSA programs recognize this reality. These offenders sometimes need incapacitation or closer monitoring, supervision, and regular meetings with community volunteers. This requires a working partnership with criminal justice professionals.

- Restorative justice is concerned with **obligations**. Once a person chooses to sexually offend, they should not necessarily have the same rights as other community members. If the offender is more focused on "rights" than their "responsibilities," restorative justice practitioners should be concerned. Offenders should strive to have empathy, change, and live healthily.

This chapter has more words about "hope" than "accountability." However, the principle, as articulated in chapter 3, is that taking responsibility happens best within a context of support. On one hand, the primary responsibility of offenders is indeed accountability. On the other hand, a restorative justice framework, where possible, encourages communities to support offenders as they do this. This can be difficult, as communities are also victimized by an offender's harmful choices; we will discuss this in the next chapter.

6

# Communities

## *A case study*

---

*S*arah was a long-time member of her church. Her nineteen-year-old son disclosed that he had been sexually molested a few years back by his youth pastor, who was still currently in the same position at the church. Sarah was sick over the news. Yet, she was proud that her son had been brave enough to share it with her. With her son's permission, she decided to divulge it to a trusted member of the church leadership team.

Unfortunately, Sarah was not believed. Even after she approached a second member of leadership, she was given a list of reasons why she—and her son—might have been mistaken. She was silenced. The youth pastor was allowed to continue in *his role. Sarah left the church, wondering if she could ever feel at home in a faith community again. Her child had been hurt, her trust had been broken, her voice had been silenced, and justice was far from her reach.*

*A few years later, Sarah was invited by a close friend to attend a different congregation. She reluctantly agreed. One week, at a small group meeting at a friend's house, Sarah shared what had happened at her previous church. This small group of people affirmed her story and validated the injustices she had faced. Sarah felt heard for the first time.*

*Two years later, she and other church members learned that one of their current church leaders had been charged (eventually convicted) with a sexual offense. The community was in shock and disarray, and Sarah began to relive some of the same feelings from years earlier. Sarah decided to leave the church. However, before doing so, she received a call from one of the elders of the church, an invitation to attend a restorative justice conference. The church, having accepted it was in crisis, proactively sought the help of professionals. Although the charged man was not accused of assaulting anyone within his church community, the leaders acknowledged that impact and the resultant needs to be addressed.*

*Like other congregants, Sarah was invited—but not obligated—to attend the restorative justice conference. It was something Sarah had never experienced before. Led by two facilitators and comprised of eight other people from her church, including the senior pastor and the wife of the man who had been charged, people were able to share their perspectives, discuss what they needed, and consider how to restore the community. Although the process was extremely difficult, through it, Sarah felt valued. She felt the freedom to express herself honestly. She also heard other perspectives, including some she had not considered before, such as that of the convicted man's wife.*

*Ultimately, the process gave her the capacity to remain in the community despite the pain and some dysfunction that was occurring around her. She felt connected instead of isolated and committed rather than disengaged. The group had direction, some ideas for moving forward. Now, six years later, Sarah is a member of a thriving church.*

## On caring for community

Unfortunately, Sarah's story is all too common. It represents the many community-based organizations, like faith communities, that are impacted by sexual abuse. It also points to the many individuals who are left feeling hurt and disconnected by the way leaders sometimes choose to respond. In many cases, organizations are not adequately prepared to navigate the pain and dysfunction. As a result, stories of sexual abuse may be doubted or managed poorly.

However, these failures do not define all situations. As we saw at the end of Sarah's story, the impacts of sexual abuse can create opportunities for resilience and growth. Sarah's story and others like it point to the reality that community-based organizations, including churches, *can* survive the impacts of a sexual offense. Many have.

This chapter will address the question, "How can a community-based organization deal with sexual abuse in its midst?" The ideas presented here speak to the need to care for community members after sexual abuse has taken place. The chapter will speak to the common impacts and needs of organizations and will include some suggestions for navigating these situations.

## Common impacts and suggested responses

When considering the impact of sexual abuse on a community-based organization, it is important to remember that each individual will respond at a personal level. For this reason, understanding the human body's common responses to trauma is vital for understanding an organization's collective response. Drawing from the field of psychosocial trauma, we know that sexual crimes are often "traumagenic," meaning they are trauma-inducing. What many people do not realize is that the ripple effects of trauma reach far beyond direct victims and may also impact people within the wider community.

In *Trauma and Recovery*, Judith Herman explains that traumagenic events often destroy, or at least disrupt, our normal sense of reality, leaving us with needs that we did not have before the trauma took place.[26] This applies at a community level, too. In the story above, it is particularly traumatic when a person in a place of authority and trust hurts someone. People question, "How could he or she have done this?" Safety, meaning-making, and reconnection are common recovery needs for communities. When trauma touches an organization, being proactive about creating a system of care for those within it is vital to its health. This cannot be done without naming the harm done.

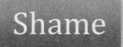

**Shame** Shame breeds secrecy; it is important for organizations to **acknowledge** sexual abuse as inappropriate and harmful. Victims' needs should be prioritized. This will begin to reestablish safety.

An experience of shame is a common response to sexual abuse within a community. Shame can be felt individually and collectively and is often experienced as a loss of respect, dignity, or self-esteem. Unfortunately, in many cases, shame results in secrecy. We saw this in the response of the elders in Sarah's first church.

Dr. James Gilligan explains why this happens as he observes that "nothing is more shameful than to feel ashamed."[27] Shame creates a loss of honor, status, respect, and a disintegration of identity. This in turn produces a need to cover, hide, and keep secrets. Shame is one reason why victims of sexual abuse may not disclose their abuse for many years—if at all—and why organizations have the tendency to hide rather than expose it. Thus, shame is one impact of sexual abuse that often perpetuates dysfunctional behavior. The tragedy is that this secrecy often enables offenders and further harms victims. When their stories are not acknowledged, victims can be re-traumatized.

Communities need to denounce sexual abuse as inappropriate and harmful. This honors victims, whose stories are often doubted, while also helping a community re-establish a sense of safety.

**Confusion**

Sexual abuse undermines a community's sense of meaning. Questions arise: How could someone do this? Who can we trust? If this is a faith community, why would God allow it? Opportunities **for asking questions** help restore a sense of meaning.

Similar to what we have described with individuals, communities struggle to make sense of sexual abuse. Confusion persists. Groups wonder how someone could have done this to another, a child, someone who is vulnerable? Why do things like this happen? Often, parents wonder if their children are safe. Whenever people are given opportunity to express hurts and confusions, groups are better able to restore a sense of meaning.

**Disconnection**

Community members will have varying reactions to sexual abuse. In a faith community, for example, some will back away from victims because they won't know how to interact with them. Disputes will arise about whether an offender should still be allowed to attend services.

People will react very differently to the disclosure of sexual abuse in a community. Many will be deeply hurt while others might minimize the harm. Some will want to support the victims; others will align with the accused. Disagreements will arise about what it means to be a part of the community. For example, some will say, regardless of what an offender has done, he or she should still be able to be a part of the group. Others will disagree. Schisms will likely arise. This is a real challenge for leadership. We would suggest that it is important to keep the harms of shame, confusion, and disconnection in mind. Those designing and leading processes should think carefully about re-establishing safety, meaning, and connection where possible.

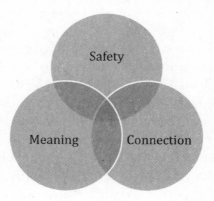

This means that leadership must find a way to act, to engage multiple—often competing—voices. In this next part, we will highlight first the type of leadership this calls for and, second, options for restorative justice processes within community groups.

Healthy leadership does not function in isolation—it asks for help from therapists, criminal justice professionals, and others about how to safely respond.

## Leadership

Leading an organization through the aftermath of sexual abuse is a significant responsibility. Indeed, leadership plays a large role in the health and life of community-based organizations. This is especially true in times of crisis.

Judith Herman and other trauma specialists have observed that our capacity for healing and resilience is based on the resources available to us. In light of this, we argue that a leader's role is to ensure the community has the resources it needs to move toward resilience and healing after a crisis of sexual abuse. Notice that we did *not* say that the leader's role was to *be* the resource; rather, the leader is meant to facilitate support and to make resources available.

The International Institute of Restorative Practices offers an image for understanding restorative leadership more clearly. In the image below (left), we see four different models for leadership. We see that working *with* the community, in a way that is both firm and fair, allows for authority and respect to co-exist and flourish together. *Firm* (or *punitive*) might be not allowing a person who has offended sexually to attend a congregation without clear boundaries. *Fair* (or *for*) could be giving opportunities for this person to share what his hopes are for ongoing involvement. *With,* in this model, suggests that "engagement" with other people is the healthiest approach to have. Remember that, through sexual abuse, victims have been disempowered. By giving them voice and choice, a leader can help victims heal.

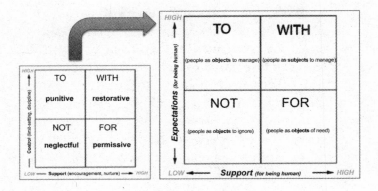

# Four leadership models[28]

Leadership will need to consider the process of intervention. What is the best way to re-establish safety, meaning, and connection for community members? In our experience, formal processes, like large group meetings (where appropriate information can be shared and people can ask questions), circle gatherings (where people can share harms and feelings), and problem-solving groups (where plans for the future can be discussed) go a long way to helping communities heal. In the chart below, we offer some questions for consideration about integrating a restorative justice framework. Remember, restorative justice is not synonymous with a particular practice but can be lived out in a variety of ways. No response will perfectly attend to everyone's feelings.

Communities also need to be self-reflective:

- **Do interventions favor the accused at the expense of victims?** The starting point of interventions is believing victims. People almost never falsely claim to having been sexually abused. They have nothing to gain by going through the difficulty of publicly disclosing such treatment.

- **Does the community need to be accountable for attitudes and beliefs that influence sexual offending?** If the community is patriarchal, promoting an unhealthy, violent version of masculinity—one that says, "Men are to be in charge"—then work needs to be done to change. Communities should consider educating boys and men about equity and the necessity of consent as it relates to human sexuality.

# Action and engagement

| Action | Description |
| --- | --- |
| What | • What is the best process for making things as right as possible?<br>• Is it a meeting about sharing feelings and impacts, or is it about problem-solving? Is it both?<br>• What information should everyone know? What information is private? What permission needs to be granted in order to share certain information? |
| How | • Do you need to ask for external help, or does your organization have the internal resources/capacity to carry out a restorative justice approach?<br>• In our experience, asking for the help of professionals is often the better choice. This does not mean defaulting responsibility for an intervention to an outsider, but sharing it. Collaboration!<br>• Forming a reference group of stakeholders (i.e., people who represent differing needs) can help.<br>• How will communication happen? Some level of transparency from leadership is important. People are already talking!<br>• Voluntary participation is a core tenet of restorative justice practice, as is discussing issues of safety in advance of any meeting. |

| | |
|---|---|
| Who | • Who needs to be involved in the discernment, design, and execution of an engagement process?<br>• Who has been affected? Not everyone will want to participate, but consideration for including, or at least inviting, everyone is paramount.<br>• Who has a *stake* in this situation—who, from the organization and community, should be involved in the process?<br>• Who should be leading processes? Trained restorative justice facilitators can help make the process safe. |
| Where | • Not only is it important to be intentional about who is involved, how they are involved, and what the process is, but *where* the process actually takes place is also critical. Places carry memory with them and impact people on a symbolic level, so choosing a safe space is important.<br>• This means that a neutral location, an equally meaningful meeting place, or (if victims are directly involved) a place where victims feel secure can foster a stronger process. |
| When | • Think about the timing of the process. Acting too soon could cause more harm, while acting too late could do the same.<br>• Much of restorative justice practice is about managing the expectations of participants along with the logistics of the process. Preparation is important. Restorative justice facilitators often meet individually with participants in advance. Is what they are hoping to accomplish feasible given the process? |

# An example: FaithCARE

One example of a restorative justice program that works with faith communities is FaithCARE.[29] It was founded in 2007 by the Shalem Mental Health Network, a Canadian mental health organization in Hamilton, Ontario. Executive Director Mark Vander Vennen was not happy with the tools and processes available for churches dealing with crises. He saw the need for developing a practice that could work more effectively in congregational settings.

Today, in addition to working with congregations preventively, FaithCARE partners with faith communities to help them through conflict, harm, and crises.

FaithCARE believes in:

- Acknowledging harm and shame.
- Doing adequate preparation to determine the appropriateness of any type of restorative justice encounter, thus ensuring safety.
- Using trained facilitators.
- Considering power imbalances, including gender . ones.
- Employing a co-facilitation model, where one facilitator is male, the other female, and one is an "insider" (representative of the faith denomination where the intervention is taking place), the other an "outsider" (not representative).
- Relying on voluntary participation.
- Using a reference team (further explained below).

Before designing an appropriate intervention, FaithCARE establishes an internal reference group consisting of church members who are aware of what has happened. Often this group is representative of leadership, like a pastor or board members, but often also includes people with differing points of view on how to handle the situation. The reference group helps the restorative justice facilitators understand the context where the intervention is taking place, who should be involved, and how to move forward in as safe a way as possible.

Typically, FaithCARE uses a restorative justice circle process, trying to involve as many people as possible—victims, offenders, leadership, others. Ground rules are established, and facilitators usually follow a script similar to the one designed by the International Institute for Restorative Practices.[30] Prior to the circle, facilitators meet with participants individually or in small groups to discuss expectations, hopes, and the kinds of questions that facilitators will be asking.

FaithCARE does acknowledge some limitations. Misconceptions about restorative justice create questions such as, "Will I be pressured to forgive?" Such misconceptions can cause reluctance to seek help from restorative justice programs. Many people don't know that restorative justice can be used as a dialogue process for community groups even when direct victims and/or offenders do not wish to participate. Sometimes there is a complicated relationship between the criminal justice system and the congregation's own process. Other limitations may be pragmatic: Can the faith community financially afford outside help?

Furthermore, people process pain at different rates; one person will take longer than another. Victims may feel pressure from their community to enter into a process when they are not ready or even willing when an offender might be. However, as Mark Vander Vennen says, "The victim should not be there to meet the offender's needs. That already happened once." FaithCARE is clear that victims should not be pressured to forgive or participate in processes against their will.

In spite of some limitations, FaithCARE opens communities to new possibilities. Anyone who has experienced harm can participate in the process of healing. Many of FaithCARE's practices, including formal restorative conferences, do not depend on the presence of a victim or offender. This acknowledges that sexual abuse impacts the larger community. Many people need space to express feelings and ask questions.

FaithCARE offers a good example of how communities can work restoratively to address sexual abuse.

# Restorative justice and sexual assault on university/college campuses

As indicated in chapter 2, sexual assault rates on university and college campuses are high. One would think that academic institutions would be places that foster equality and respect for others. In some ways, they do. Yet, incidents of male-perpetrated sexual violence are especially high at the outset of the academic year, when toxic masculinity is allowed to flourish.[31] Part of the restorative justice work that needs to be done is addressing patriarchal, male violence more systematically. The other is responding restoratively, where possible, to individual incidents.

The first steps of a restorative justice response are: believing victims, ensuring physical and emotional safety, and helping them move toward healing. The next steps involve encouraging individual offenders to take responsibility while also examining components of university/college culture that promote rape and other forms of male violence. Mary Koss, a long-time expert on how to respond safely and appropriately to sexual abuse, has written with colleagues Jay Wilgus and Kaaren Williamsen about using restorative justice with sexual misconduct cases on campuses.[32] These authors see a number of possibilities for a restorative justice framework in campus sexual misconduct cases:

1.  **Restorative justice as a resolution process.**
    This option is intended to give victims a choice for a possible resolution through safe, facilitated restorative justice dialogue. Participants must go through

adequate preparation stages, including locating supports for all parties. Outcomes typically include a redress plan with the following components:

- Reparations
- Counseling
- Community service
- Mandatory supervision

If restorative justice is to be used as a resolution process, it should not be termed "mediation." One party, the offender, has caused harm to another, the victim, and therefore the parties do not enter neutrally. Restorative justice names wrongdoing, acknowledges harm, and promotes accountability.

2. **Restorative justice as a sanctioning process.**
   If an offender is found to be responsible, whether an offender admits to guilt or not, Koss et al. see a role for victims and other community members in the sanctioning process. The authors suggest that forms of separation are necessary at times: temporary suspension and/or permanent expulsion. Including victims and community members in this process is not intended to put an extra burden on them but rather to determine what is needed for safety and healing.

3. **Restorative justice as a reintegration process.**
   With this option, a responsible offender, after fulfilling conditions of a suspension, is safely reintegrated back into a campus community. The dual purposes of restorative justice reintegration

are support and accountability. Like the Circles of Support and Accountability program, it honors the offender as a human being while still ensuring ongoing safety on the campus.

In addition, we would also see restorative justice as a way to engage the broader community about harm and healing. Inviting community input acknowledges the problem of gender-based violence on campuses. Sexual violence affects all students, particularly women and transgendered people. The wider community, especially men, has an obligation to transform rape culture into a consent- and equity-based culture.

In conclusion, this chapter continues to promote restorative justice as a framework, rather than a particular set of practices. Strong community leadership is needed to ensure that victims are safe, offenders are accountable, and root causes of sexual abuse are addressed.

7

# An Indigenous Community

## *A case study*

---

The Ojibwe, or Anishinaabe, People of Hollow
Water First Nation on Turtle Island (in the area
known today as Manitoba, Canada) provide an
exemplar for how to respond restoratively to sexual
abuse. Hollow Water is a story of hope through trauma.

In the mid–1980s, this indigenous community was
facing a crisis. It was estimated that, of the approximately 600 people, 3 out of 4 had been victims of sexual
abuse while 1 in 3 were perpetrators.[33] Widespread

sexual abuse in Hollow Water was also a story of intergenerational trauma, starting with Canada's violent colonization of indigenous peoples. The Indian Act and other colonial practices assimilated rather than honored indigenous sovereignty. Canadian law legalized land theft and displaced indigenous peoples to small, often useless tracts of land called reserves. Colonial practices like residential schools removed children from communities such as Hollow Water and decimated indigenous societies. The history of Indian residential schools, in particular, is important for understanding how intergenerational violence became commonplace in Hollow Water.

Throughout one hundred years of Canada's history, up until 1996, from one side of the country to the other, over 150,000 indigenous children were forcibly removed from their communities into almost 150 Indian residential schools. The explicit purpose was to "kill the Indian in the Child."[34] Not allowed to speak their languages, nor practice their traditions, and given a number instead of a name, the schools were a form of cultural genocide. Sexual and physical abuses by teachers, priests, and other so-called caregivers ran rampant. Cultural, physical, and sexual violence translated into generation upon generation of indigenous children who grew up and were unable to parent properly. Physical and sexual abuse was repeated in their homes. In a report by the Truth and Reconciliation Commission on Indian residential schools in Canada titled *They Came for the Children*, the child of a residential school survivor said, "We didn't really escape [residential school] either. It visited us everyday of our childhood through the replaying over and over of our parents' trauma and grief which they never had the opportunity to resolve in their lifetimes."[35] In the words

70

of Crown Attorney Rupert Ross, writing in *Returning to the Teachings: Exploring Aboriginal Justice*, "[R]esidential schools were not the solitary cause of social breakdown amongst aboriginal people. Rather, they were the punctuation mark in a loud, long declaration that nothing aboriginal could possibly be of value to anyone. That message had been delivered in every way imaginable, and it touched every aspect of traditional social organization."[36] Although it is difficult to put into words how devastating colonization was and continues to be, indigenous communities and traditions have survived.

In 1984, with Hollow Water exhausted by epidemic sexual abuse, several community leaders breathed life into the community with a plan to heal. Drawing on their traditional indigenous ways, the Community Holistic Circle Healing (CHCH) program was formed.

The CHCH took control of the healing process. Part of what was taken during colonization was indigenous sovereignty over justice processes. The CHCH contended that interventions by the Canadian criminal justice system had only caused further harm. Prior to colonization, when harm occurred, the Ojibwe of Hollow Water would focus efforts toward healing and integration, not punishment and separation. In fact, the CHCH argued that traditional healing was a much more serious way to deal with sexual abuse: "The people of Hollow Water do not believe in incarceration. They believe that incarceration means that offenders can hide from, rather than face, their responsibilities for the pain they have caused. The difference in Hollow Water is that offenders face their responsibilities with the love, respect, and support which the Anishinaabe people believe are due to all creatures."[37] So, the CHCH established healing circles for victims, healing circles for offenders, and healing circles where victims and offenders could be brought together in dialogue. Participation was voluntary. For example, if an offender denied responsibility, he or she could instead go through the Canadian criminal justice system.

Surprisingly—or perhaps not, from an indigenous perspective—with the establishment of the CHCH, some offenders even came forward to report their crimes. About this Ross says:

> [T]hey had offenders come forward and disclose their abusive behaviour *on their own*, asking for help for everyone. As a Crown Attorney, I can honestly say that no one has ever walked into my office and said, 'I want to confess that I sexually abused my stepdaughter, please prosecute me.' To the extent that sexual abuse spreads from one generation to the next as long as silence is maintained . . . our emphasis on punishment, by contributing to silence, may also be encouraging the continuation of abuse.[38]

In a position paper on the topic, the CHCH claimed that the threat of incarceration silences offenders and therefore causes further suffering to victims and harm to communities: "It reinforces the silence and therefore promotes, rather than breaks, the cycle of violence that exists. In reality, rather than making the community a safer place, the threat of jail places the community more at risk."[39] Instead of the avoidance and denial perpetuated by the criminal justice system, the CHCH promoted accountability.

However, the main focus of the CHCH program was supporting victims. It was a 13-stage process:

1. Disclosure.
2. Establish Safety for the Victim.

3. Confront the Victimizer.
4. Support the Spouse/Parent.
5. Support the Family(ies)/Community.
6. Meeting of Assessment Team with Royal Canadian Mounted Police.
7. Circles with Victimizer.
8. Circles with Victim and Victimizer.
9. Prepare Victim's Family.
10. Prepare Victimizer's Family.
11. Special Gather/Sentencing Circle.
12. Sentencing Review.
13. Cleansing Ceremony.[40]

The focus was on helping to restore balance, following seven traditional teachings, and working toward healing all aspects of a person's life: emotional, mental, spiritual, and physical. One of the leaders of CHCH, Joyce Bushie, said:

> The seven sacred teachings are honesty, strength, respect, caring, sharing, wisdom, and humility. These were the teachings Creator gave the Aboriginal people to follow. Some call it the guideline to life. To be honest, we need to work on the four aspects of our being emotionally, mentally, spiritually and physically. Without the four, then we can't function as whole human beings. That's why we need the Sacred Circles and the seven teachings to begin to heal the scars of the ancestors.[41]

Did the community heal? Not only were traditional teachings brought to the fore, the engagement with offenders worked. Of the 107 that went through the CHCH process, only two sexually re-offended, a rate of less than 2%.[42] Compared to the Canadian criminal

73

justice system, which averages a 13% recidivism rate for sex offenders, the CHCH data is impressive.[43]

## Lessons learned

There are a number of lessons that restorative justice practitioners can learn from Hollow Water.

1. **Sexual abuse does not happen in isolation.**

   In previous chapters, we've documented that sexual abuse is most often a form of gender-based violence, perpetrated by men. In this chapter, the colonization of indigenous peoples was linked to sexual abuse. Furthermore, state-based criminal justice responses separate victims from offenders. Of course, this is often necessary for the safety of the victim. In the Hollow Water context, however, the separation of victim from offender further damaged the community as sexual abuse was an insidious part of most families' lives.

2. **Fear of punishment can contribute to cycles of sexual abuse.**

   Victims often do not come forward for fear of being doubted or ignored. Likewise, the case of Hollow Water hints at fear of punishment as a barrier to offenders' taking responsibility.

3. **Criminal justice responses often further damage certain racial communities.**

   Research indicates that most sexual offenders belong to society's dominant groups, yet racial and other minorities are overwhelmingly targeted by law enforcement. In *The Four Circles of Hollow Water*, researcher Christine Sivell-Ferri argues,

"[I]t is apparent that some sexual offenders are members of minority groups but most belong to society's predominant groups. Reporting, and the subsequent investigative and judicial processes, tend to be biased toward identifying and incarcerating those sexual offenders who come from either lower income or minority backgrounds, but this should not be taken as evidence that such groups produce more sexual offenders."[44] In fact, the propensity to disproportionately incarcerate minorities is visible in the wider social context. In Canada, indigenous peoples represent almost 25% of inmates while only comprising 3% of the general population.[45] In the United States, African American, Latino, and Native Americans make up the majority of inmates in prisons even though they are minorities within the general population.

Restorative justice practices offer a promising solution. The approach of Hollow Water put power in the hands of the community to respond in the way that was most appropriate to it. However, law enforcement, courts, and prisons provided an alternative backdrop that offenders could also choose. Not only did this give more attention to the needs of victims and provide safety for children, it also fostered community development and the advancement of traditions important to the Ojibwe people.

## 4. Restorative justice as social justice.

The story of Hollow Water indicates that, when power is put in the hands of communities to address their problems, restorative justice responses can function as an intervention and a preventive mechanism. Some "standpoints" who articulate the need for voice and control for women and marginalized races in justice processes are hopeful about the social justice possibilities of restorative justice. In the article "Restorative Justice as Social Justice for Victims of Gendered Violence: A Standpoint Feminist Perspective," author Katherine van Wormer claimed that the adversarial criminal justice system is often experienced as "white justice" and is therefore foreign to African American, Latino, and indigenous peoples.[46] Restorative justice gives voice—making victims subjects rather than objects—to participants in defining how to meet justice needs, and heal.

**5. Justice processes, where stolen, need to be returned.**

Colonialism in Canada—and the United States—installed its own justice processes and eviscerated those of indigenous societies, contributing to the intergenerational traumas of indigenous peoples. Many indigenous societies are fighting for self-determination, for a sovereignty that was never fully restored. Although it is a partnership between a Western and an indigenous system, the CHCH highlights what might be possible when the power to carry out justice is returned to a community. Furthermore, while the case study highlights how the indigenous community took responsibility for its healing, Canada and the US must also take the initiative to decolonize—for example, by returning to indigenous peoples what has been taken and to honor treaties.

8

# Limits and
# Possibilities

The application of restorative justice to sexual
violence has been a controversial topic. The
resulting dialogue among academics and
practitioners has highlighted some of the limits
and challenges and yet, at the same time, fresh
possibilities. In this chapter, we will explore some of the
concerns or necessary limits, as well as the possibilities,
that restorative justice offers.

# Limits

### 1. One-size-fits-all

Many people do not know what restorative justice is or, if they do, are not well informed. Some think it is a set of practices, equating it with victim-offender dialogue. Others think that it forces victims to forgive or reconcile with offenders or that it is "soft" on crime. Some of these misconceptions have understandably emerged from misapplications of restorative justice. To date, in North America, restorative justice practices have largely centered on some form of victim-offender dialogue, and some have erroneously promoted reconciliation. Restorative justice programs need to be cautious about becoming a one-size-fits-all approach. Our hope is that we have been able to position restorative justice as a philosophy, one that puts victims' needs at the forefront of justice processes. Keeping this in mind should help practitioners implement it in ways that meet the complex needs of victims, offenders, and communities.

### 2. Safety

Another concern about restorative justice dialogue is the potential for harm when inappropriately used or conducted. As Judith Herman makes clear, meeting justice needs depends first on establishing safety. Since sexual abuse often involves power imbalances, dialogue may be inappropriate. At the very least, it must be done cautiously (i.e., with significant preparation), paying attention to safety and power imbalances.

Victims and all other participants need to be able to make an informed choice about participation. One component of this is being clear about expectations. Does a victim want to share how his or her life has been affected? What if the offender acknowledges guilt but does not vocalize recognition of the full impact? Does a victim want an apology? What if an offender is willing to say "sorry" but not to do the hard work of understanding why he committed an offense? Practitioners need to be adequately versed in preparing victims and offenders for the potential pitfalls of this type of process.

Furthermore, restorative justice practitioners should be trauma-informed—that is, have an understanding of how trauma affects people and how best to support resilience.

### 3. Social justice

An important critique of restorative justice is that many programs do not adequately address underlying social pressures, norms, and injustices. In other words, programs do not get at systemic issues because they are focused on the individuals at hand. What happens if restorative justice is only used as an intervention and ignores root causes? When dealing with sexual abuse in particular, a gendered analysis is invaluable to this conversation. This perspective acknowledges that social issues like sexual violence cannot be understood without also considering the social, historical, and cultural construction of gender. Still, taking into account sexual abuse as a social issue, an experience, *and* a crime, restorative justice is potentially an incomplete solution to the problem.

Is it possible that restorative justice over-individualizes wrongs that have significant roots in underlying structures? Could this be a repetition of the criminal justice system's approach to dealing with individual crimes rather than underlying structures? Can restorative justice be a way to transform structures? Or could it be a movement toward a more transformative approach that will eventually address social issues? The restorative justice versus "transformative" justice debate is ongoing in the restorative justice field.

## 4. Extra-legal

Another critique of restorative justice is that it is often "extra-legal," or outside the formal criminal justice system. Some programs, especially ones for youth, are often diversionary. Still, the criminal justice system plays an important role in denouncing wrongdoing. Some have asked: "If gendered violence is not formally treated as crime in the court of law, are we taking a step backward instead of forward?" The concern is that, by privatizing this issue or by utilizing community-based responses, restorative justice makes this issue less serious.

However, this book advocates a restorative justice approach that is open to partnership with the criminal justice system. The Restorative Opportunities program is an example.

Furthermore, restorative justice is not limited to diversionary or victim-offender encounters. Some programs are using a partial restorative justice framework, for example, by offering supports to one side or the other. Restorative justice can function in a complementary fashion to more traditional approaches, thereby meeting the justice needs of participants in ways that other approaches cannot.

## 5. Resources

An important limitation concerns funding—i.e., restorative justice practices are limited by economics. Because current spending favors existing structures and policies of criminal justice, restorative justice is often limited by dependency on unstable sources. Canada, for example, has written restorative justice options into legislation governing young offenders but has not made available sufficient resources for actually implementing this programming. Furthermore, crime continues to be a political issue in the Western world. Many politicians are reluctant to take a stand outside of "tough on crime" policies. With politics as a bellwether, resources are channeled toward items like prison maintenance or expansion rather than toward practices considered "alternative" such as restorative justice. What is more, given already scarce resources, some are concerned that such programs will move funding away from other important victim services.

# Possibilities

## 1. Healthy alternatives

In spite of such challenges or limits, there are many reasons for optimism. Many victims of sexual abuse have found their experiences with the criminal justice system to be disempowering and re-traumatizing. For this reason, some victims of sexual crimes choose an alternative approach that gives them more voice, choice, and power. Overall, restorative justice offers more options for meeting the diverse needs of victims. Different victim/offender relationships, as well as differing victim needs, can be taken into account in restorative justice processes.

## 2. Validation

A restorative justice process should be set up to validate victims' needs: believing their stories, assuring safety, giving their questions priority, offering them options, and so on. Restorative justice processes provide assurance to victims that they are not to blame for the violence they experienced. A dialogue process—be it a victim-offender conference or a family group conference as in New Zealand's juvenile justice system[47]—can also validate victims' needs and experiences in a way that the criminal justice system does not.

> Restorative justice processes can validate victims' needs & experiences in a way that the criminal justice system does not.

The same can be said for accountability: restorative justice processes encourage the taking of responsibility and an admission of wrongs in a way that the criminal justice system does not. In the legal process, offenders are often encouraged to deny their offenses and plead not guilty. This denial increases the hurt experienced by victims and points offenders away from the impact of their actions and their obligation to take responsibility. In restorative justice conferences, offenders often take fuller responsibility as they begin to understand the impact of their behavior. Further, victims can avoid public humiliation, finding instead heightened esteem, validation, respect, dignity, and personal power.

## 3. Choice and decision-making

The opportunity for victims to choose what they need and *how* they want to attain justice encourages recovery in that it meets their needs for power and autonomy as well as safety. Restorative justice offers victims more voice in decision-making—from how the process takes place to when it takes place to who is involved and to what s/he thinks the outcomes should be. In this way, victims are able to choose both what they need and how they will attain it.

When an offender is caught and admits wrongdoing, restorative justice dialogue can create new possibilities for victim empowerment. Even when there is no arrest, some restorative justice programs are helping victims dialogue with family members or offering ongoing peer supports (e.g., see Community Justice Initiatives program above).

### 4. Opportunity for dialogue

Another unique and significant possibility restorative justice processes provide is the potential for dialogue between parties. Of course, dialogue is not appropriate in every case, but some victims have a desire to speak directly to their offenders, especially in serious offenses where victims are left wanting answers. Victims are able to ask questions, but they are also able to tell their stories and talk about effects.

By participating in a restorative justice encounter, victims and their communities are also able to condemn violence in a meaningful way for all parties involved. Furthermore, restorative justice processes are not limited to direct victims and offenders. Sometimes victims find it helpful to meet with "surrogate" offenders—offenders who have committed similar offenses. Conversely, it is often helpful for sex offenders to hear from and dialogue with victims that they did not harm themselves but who have experienced the crime at the hands of others. More opportunities for dialogue can be created when communities can share impacts and collaborate on how to move forward.

### 5. Hope and inclusion

Restorative justice is inclusive. Victims are people. Sex offenders are people. Each matter, and each belong, in some way, in our communities. Inclusion does not mean we minimize harm or eliminate boundaries. If a person who has offended sexually cannot live within the boundaries of respectful relationships, then incapacitation or separation is appropriate. However, in adopting a restorative justice ethos, we choose to live with hope: the hope that harms can be meaningfully addressed and that everyone can be given proper support and care to move toward healing.

| Limits | Possibilities |
|---|---|
| • One-size-fits-all. | • Increases range of choices for victims. |
| • Safety considerations for victims must be taken into account. | • Recognizes unique cases. |
| • Language can be a barrier—e.g., "victims" or "restoration." | • Encourages admissions of offending, rather than denial. |
| • May not adequately address underlying social causes. | • Processes can contribute to healing through narrating, being heard, and getting answers to questions. |
| • Message sent with diversion might diminish the gravity of sexual abuse and its gendered nature. | • Offers a dialogue encounter, a transformative and meaningful way of denouncing violence. |
| • Economics of the practice and politicizing of crime. | • Based on more holistic and common views of crime, more inclusive, offering hope. |

We believe it is important to acknowledge the limits of restorative justice. Its practices, at present, are not a complete method for responding to the issue of sexual abuse, nor does everyone desire this type of approach. However, it is also clear to us that this avenue of justice meets many of the needs of victims and calls sex offenders to a new level of accountability. Although the field or practice is not perfect, restorative justice offers victims, offenders, and their communities new possibilities for finding justice after sexual abuse has taken place.

Although restorative justice as currently practiced is not applicable to every situation, we would argue that the restorative justice framework is. Who has been hurt in this situation? What are their needs? What are the obligations, and whose are they? What are the underlying causes? Who needs to be involved? And what are the best processes to address these questions? We dream of the day when these questions are routinely asked.

9

# Principled
# Practice

The size of this Little Book does not allow detailed discussion of specific programs and models. The models outlined in several other books in this series do suggest possibilities though. These are listed in "Suggested Reading" in the appendix.

Rather than specific program models, we advocate "principled practice"—practice that arises from key values. The principles and values of restorative justice, as outlined in *The Little Book of Restorative Justice*, provide one set. These nine principles offer guidance to restorative responses to sexual violence.

### Principle 1: Victims first

- The first priority is always safety. In addition to physical safety, part of this is allowing victims the space *and* time to identify their needs. This will sometimes come at the expense of offenders' needs, and that needs to be okay. Victims take precedence.

### Principle 2: Trauma-informed

- Sexual abuse is most often experienced as traumatic. Any intervention needs to consider how a victim experiences trauma. Many offenders also have histories of trauma: what does it mean to hold them accountable within a context of support? Trauma-informed means that practices should attempt to do no further harm. Trauma-informed means a focus on strengths, resilience, and hope.

### Principle 3: Structural analysis

- Interventions must consider the big picture. Why are men more likely to offend sexually than women? Why are indigenous people and people of color in North America more likely to be incarcerated than white people? Why are people with mental health challenges and addiction issues overrepresented in prisons? Why are people living in poverty arrested more often than those of the middle or upper classes? How are these factored into restorative justice interventions?

## Principle 4: Inclusive within limits

- Everyone has the right to be a part of a community. However, inclusion in a community implies maintenance of respect for each other; when someone has offended sexually, they have given this up, in part. Communities need to carefully consider how they will welcome sex offenders. Just because a person has "served their time" does not mean they should not be restricted from certain activities. Faith communities, in particular, often struggle with this. What are the appropriate boundaries for including someone in a community?

## Principle 5: Silence is not golden

- The best way to stop sexual abuse from happening is to talk about it. Violence thrives on secrecy. Efforts toward prevention need to consider how children can be better taught about these difficult issues. Interventions, too, must not shy away from naming harm. Facilitators of restorative justice have responsibilities to multiple stakeholders, victims, offenders, and communities. They also have a responsibility to stand against violence. Restorative justice is not neutral about this.

## Principle 6: Community responsibility

- Communities experience the harm of sexual abuse. Family members are deeply hurt when one of their own has been sexually abused. Members of a community experience betrayal and other pain when news of offending in their midst is exposed. These needs must be attended.

- At the same time, communities have a responsibility to care for their members and to prevent future harms. If we are to get at the root causes of sexual abuse, we must find ways to talk about it in schools, community centers, faith communities, and homes. The community must own this responsibility.

## Principle 7: Informed voluntary participation

- People need to be given choices. Regardless of the formality of the intervention, do participants understand the process, expectations, responsibilities, boundaries, etc.? If an offender is not taking full responsibility prior to a restorative conference, should the victim know this in order to make an informed choice about participation? Restorative justice does not force people to participate, even when community members think they should. If participation is compelled, processes would be counterproductive.

## Principle 8: Preparation matters

- This principle speaks to the need for adequate preparation. The more formal the process, the more preparation necessary. Having trained facilitators can help with this. Facilitators must take the time to meet individually (or in small groups) with everyone prior to any sort of dialogue. Further, co-facilitation is better than individual facilitation in these situations.
- Part of this is an assessment: Is it safe/appropriate to bring these participants together? Are their needs too divergent, or is their

sufficient convergence to proceed? What are the intentions, objectives, goals, and hopes of participants? Do they understand the limits and possibilities of the process? What would they like to say? What would they like to ask? Do they have the capacity to participate meaningfully? What supports do willing participants need in order to be at their best?

**Principle 9: Appropriate partnerships**
- Restorative justice interventions should not function in isolation. In our experience, it is often helpful to include therapists and criminal justice professionals, such as probation officers, in community dialogue processes. Furthermore, facilitators have a responsibility to share information with the appropriate authorities if they suspect harm has been committed to a minor or will be committed to another person.
- If offenders are reluctant to take responsibility and are prone to manipulating a process, it is helpful to get written permission to discuss their case with other professionals aware of the situation. Also, where victims are involved and have a counselor, it is useful to get written consent to discuss the idea of restorative justice with their supporters.

These nine principles can be viewed as foundational building blocks for applying a restorative justice framework to sexual abuse. The principles stand on values of respect and integrity. In turn, they give shape to practice. Our book articulates this mid-level, emphasizing that restorative justice is first a principled approach and only secondarily a form of practice. In our final chapter, we will conclude by sharing a case story that highlights this.

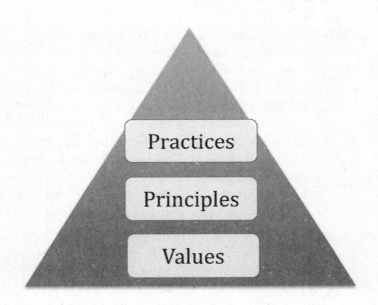

10

# Conclusion

## *A case story*

---

This story about restorative justice in response to sexual abuse highlights some of the difficulty, alongside the possibility and hope, offered by the framework articulated in this book. We emphasize: No process is perfect.

Although the following case story is based on an actual restorative justice conference, names and identifying characteristics have been changed to protect the privacy of participants.

*In a few minutes, Greg will walk into a room of twelve family members. His elderly parents are there. He imagines the consternation on their aged faces. He's never talked to his mom or his dad about this. Three sisters, one brother, their spouses, and a therapist will be in that room. How can he look at them? He would give anything to be somewhere else, anywhere else— even being in prison would be better than this, he muses. One of the restorative justice facilitators speaks.*

*"Are you ready?"*

*He looks toward a woman and a man sitting before him. A window behind the facilitator casts a shadow across her calmly reassuring face.*

*"As ready as . . . as I'll ever be," Greg replies.*

*"Is there anything else you need before we go in?" the male facilitator asks in a voice that sounds kindly to Greg's ears.*

*"No. I think we should do this now. Let's go in."*

*The facilitators get up, open the door, and point across the hall: "We're in that room. Your family is waiting."*

*. . . . . . . . .*

*Two years prior, a young woman in her late twenties, Dina, had walked into a restorative justice agency to meet with two staff members to discuss confronting her brother. He had sexu-ally abused her when he was a teenager and she was younger than ten. Her life was currently a mess, she said. She'd just ended a long-term relationship, lost her job, and had very little support from anyone in her immediate family. She wanted her life back. She wanted her family back. She wanted them to know what Greg had done.*

## Conclusion

*The facilitators provided compassionate listening and some education about trauma. They could see that Dina was very much reliving her experiences of abuse as if they were happening in the present. They asked if she had ever done counseling. She had not. After making a few phone calls, the facilitators were able to connect Dina with two counseling agencies, one where she could attend individual therapy and another offering group support. Throughout the next year, the facilitators kept in touch with Dina as she attended these programs.*

*A year later, Dina returned. She was eager to carry on with the restorative justice process. Her relationships with family members were still tenuous, and she wanted them to understand what she had been through. And she really wanted acknowledgement from Greg that he had sexually abused her, that what he had done was wrong. She also wanted to know "Why?"— What was he thinking at the time? The therapist came with Dina to her meetings with the facilitators. After six months and numerous meetings, everyone agreed that the time was right for the facilitators to contact Greg and the other family members, to see if they would consent to participating in a family meeting.*

*After some waffling, Greg agreed. He was initially concerned about legal implications but decided he'd carried this secret for too long and wanted to face his sister, his family, and any of the resulting consequences. The family, too, agreed to participate. His parents struggled to understand how something like this could have so much effect on Dina. They just wanted her to forgive Greg. Others were furious. Greg's brother felt betrayed— he'd always looked up to him, they'd done everything together growing up. Greg's older sister thought the restorative justice conference was a bad idea—she thought Dina should just go to the police. However, she wanted to be there to support her sister.*

..........

95

*Everyone is seated in a circle, no table in the center. After discussing ground rules and reminding participants why they are there, the facilitators ask everyone to briefly describe their main hope for the day. Taking turns around the circle, people speak.*

*"I want Dina to know we believe her," says one.*

*"I'm hoping that somehow, in some way, people will still be able to accept me," Greg reveals, "that all of you would know how sorry I am . . . I'm so sorry . . . so sorry . . . I hope I'll be able to look at you, that you'll be able to look at me again."*

*"I don't even know what to say, I just, I just want us to be a family again . . . that . . . that . . . Greg you disgust me," a man barks, breathing deeply.*

*"I'm hoping that Greg will hear me, that he'll know how much he hurt me, how hard it has been to live with this. I want all of you to stop judging my life and to know why I've struggled. I want my family back," Dina asserts calmly and quietly, exuding confidence and courage.*

*Facilitators guide the conversation, through what happened in the past toward how people have been affected, especially Dina. She describes the nightmare of it, how for many years it haunted her and seemed to get in the way of everything—relationships, work, and being around the family, specifically when Greg was present. She looks at him through much of the conversation. Sometimes she cries, but mostly she is poised. She worked many months with her therapist and facilitators, saying many times that she didn't think that it was hers to carry any-more—she wanted to give it back to him. Greg makes limited eye contact. He sobs. He nods. He mumbles, "Sorry."*

*The family responds. They affirm Dina and thank her for her courage. They say they are sorry for pushing her away when she was struggling. They wonder what they can do differently.*

*Greg speaks. He admits to sexually abusing Dina. He says at the time it was just play, like show-and-tell. He knew it was wrong though. He knew because he made her swear never to tell anyone. He knew because of the weight of his conscience, many decades of weight. He never realized, though, how much he had hurt her. The facilitators had challenged him during pre-conference preparation to think about it, but he hadn't truly grasped the impact until hearing her words.*

*"What can I do? 'Sorry' seems so . . . so . . . like a word, an empty word."*

*"You're here," responds Dina.*

*The facilitators move the discussion forward, essentially asking, "What needs to happen to make things as right as possible?" Things get heated for a bit. One of the sibling's spouses storms out, saying it is too much for him. The facilitators pause the process and check in with everyone. Collectively, they decide to proceed without him. However, many hours have gone by, and participants are exhausted; they decide to convene for a second meeting the following week. Dina knows she wants Greg to do some counseling, and she knows she wants to talk about family gatherings going forward.*

*Their mom has been fairly quiet throughout. Through tears, she speaks: "I never could have imagined that this was happening in our home, our beautiful home. We were so committed to taking care of each other, to being loving, to being happy. I came here wanting to brush it away, wanting everyone to forgive, to move on, and to get over it. Now I'm realizing it is going to take time. I've always told people to forgive. Now I'm not sure how to do it myself. I'm angrier than when I first got here—but happy. No, that's not the right word. Glad. So proud of you, Dina, proud that we as a family can talk about this. It changes everything—how I see you, Greg, what I think about you. But you're both my children."*

*In closing, the facilitators ask each participant to share how they are feeling as they leave.*

*"Tired. But content." Heads nod.*

*"Sad."*

*"Admiration for Dina. Glad that Greg came to the meeting."*

*"Hopeful."*

..........

Participants were satisfied with the restorative justice process and outcomes. Dina regained the support of her family, who were now able to see her current challenges through the lens of her victimization. Greg committed to counseling. Some family members distanced themselves from Greg. They were appreciative of his willingness to take responsibility but were unable to reconcile who they thought he was with what he had done. Others maintained strong, vibrant connections with him. For the first time in many years, Dina was comfortable attending family functions when Greg was present. With Greg in counseling, Dina was less worried that he might sexually abuse others.

Clearly, some significant needs had been met—for acknowledgment, for validation—as the family moved toward healing. Not all restorative justice processes will conclude like this one. In other cases, facilitators might end a process during preparation. Perhaps an offender is unwilling to move beyond minimizing crimes. Maybe a victim needs other supports, such as counseling, that better attend to his or her needs. However, this case highlights what is possible. It does not diminish the pain: there is no easy resolution. People need safe spaces to be able to grieve suffering caused by sexual abuse. In Dina's and Greg's story, the victim walked away feeling empowered, better able to face life. The offender was less burdened, the load of secrecy and shame lightened. All in all, it was not perfect but still a largely positive outcome: hope through trauma.

## Endings and beginnings

Thank you for reading this book. Our goal is to offer it as part of an ongoing conversation about the usefulness of restorative justice as a response to sexual abuse. We have been careful to write with a voice of invitation rather than one of authority. As a reader, you may disagree with points, and that is okay. The ethos of restorative justice is, in part, about creating safe space for dialogue about difficult subjects. Sexual abuse *is* a difficult subject. We hope our book makes one small contribution to ending this form of violence and to creating communities where all can belong with safety, respect, and dignity.

# ENDNOTES

[1] Judith L. Herman, *Trauma and Recovery: The Aftermath of Violence— From Domestic Abuse to Political Terror* (New York: Basic Books, 1997).

[2] Paul E. Mullen and David M. Fergusson, *Child Sexual Abuse: An Evidence-Based Perspective* (London: Sage Publications Inc., 1999).

[3] For a helpful primer on Cognitive Behavioral Therapy and its uses with addictions see: Julian Somers, *Cognitive Behavioural Therapy* (Vancouver: Centre for Applied Research in Addiction & Mental Health, 2007).

[4] Jay Harrison and Ginette Lafrenière, *The Change Project: University Campuses Ending Gendered Violence—Final Report and Recommendations to Wilfrid Laurier University* (Waterloo: Social Innovation Research Group, 2015).

[5] *ibid*

[6] Bonnie Fisher, Francis T. Cullen, and Michael G. Turner, *The Sexual Victimization of College Women* (Washington, DC: National Institute of Justice, 2000).

[7] *ibid*

[8] For example, Neil M. Malamuth, "Rape Proclivity Among Males," *Journal of Social Issues* 37, no. 4 (1981): 138–157; Julie A. Osland, Marguerite Fitch, and Edmond E. Willis, "Likelihood to Rape in College Males," *Sex Roles: A Journal of Research* 35, no. 3–4 (1996): 171–183.

[9] Brené Brown, "The Power of Vulnerability," June 2010, lecture video and transcript, 20:19, TEDxHouston, TED Talks, http://www.ted.com/talks/brene_brown_on_vulnerability.html.

[10] Brentin Mock, "Holder: 'We Can't Incarcerate Our Way to Becoming a Safer Nation,'" *Color Lines: News for Action,* August 12, 2013, http://colorlines.com/archives/2013/08/holder_we_cant_incarcerate_our_way_to_becoming_a_safer_nation.html.

[11] Brené Brown, "The Power of Vulnerability."

[12] Herman, *Trauma & Recovery: The Aftermath of Violence—From Domestic Abuse to Political Terror.*

[13] Kathleen Daly, "Restorative Justice and Sexual Assault," *British Journal of Criminology* 46, no. 2 (2006): 334–356.

[14] Clare McGlynn, Nicole Westmarland, and Nikki Godden, "'I Just Wanted Him to Hear Me': Sexual Violence and the Possibilities of Restorative Justice," *Journal of Law and Society* 39, no. 2 (2012): 213–240.

[15] Tinneke Van Camp and Jo-Anne Wemmers, "Victim Satisfaction with Restorative Justice: More Than Simply Procedural Justice," *International Review of Victimology* 19, no. 2 (2013): 117–143.

[16] National Center for Missing & Exploited Children, http://www.missingkids.com.

[17] Dennis A. Challeen, *Making It Right: A Common Sense Approach to Criminal Justice* (Aberdeen: Melius & Peterson Publishing Co., 1986), 37–39.

[18] Martin E. P. Seligman, *Learned Optimism: How to Change Your Mind and Your Life* (New York: Random House, 1990).

[19] Linda Pressly, "The Village Where Half the Population Are Sex Offenders," *BBC News Magazine,* July 31, 2013, http://www.bbc.com/news/magazine-23063492.

[20] Correctional Service of Canada, *Circles of Support & Accountability: Project Guide* (Ottawa: Correctional Service of Canada, 2003).

[21] *ibid*

[22] Marian V. Liautaud, "Sex Offenders in the Pew: How Churches Are Ministering to Society's Most Despised," *Christianity Today,* September 17, 2010, http://www.christianitytoday.com/ct/2010/september/21.49.html.

[23] Robin J. Wilson, Janice E. Picheca, and Michelle Prinzo, *Circles of Support & Accountability: An Evaluation of the Pilot Project in South-Central Ontario,* research report R-168 (Ottawa: Correctional Service of Canada, 2005).

24 Mechtild Hoing, Stefan Bogaerts, and Bas Vogelvang, "Circles of Support & Accountability: How and Why They Work for Sex Offenders," *Journal of Forensic Psychology Practice* 13, no. 4 (2013): 267–295.

25 Alan Jenkins, *Becoming Ethical: A Parallel Political Journey with Men Who Have Abused* (Dorset: Russell House Publishing, 2009).

26 Herman, *Trauma and Recovery: The Aftermath of Violence—From Domestic Abuse to Political Terror.*

27 James Gilligan, *Violence: Reflections on a National Epidemic* (New York: Vintage, 1997): 111.

28 Both images are taken from Dorothy Vaandering, *A Window on Relationships: Enlarging the Social Discipline Window for a Broader Perspective,* October 14, 2010, presentation, 13th World Conference of the International Institute of Restorative Practices, http://www.iirp.edu/pdf/Hull-2010/Hull-2010-Vaandering.pdf.

29 Shalem Mental Health Network, "FaithCARE," http://shalemnetwork.org/support-programs/support-programs-restorative-practice/faithcare/.

30 Terry O'Connell, Ben Wachtel, and Ted Wachtel, *Conferencing Handbook: The New Real Justice Training Manual* (Bethlehem: International Institute for Restorative Practices, 1999). See also International Institute for Restorative Practices, "Restorative Conference Facilitator Script," April 20, 2010, http://www.iirp.edu/article_detail.php?article_id=NjYy.

31 Harrison and Lafrenière, *The Change Project: University Campuses Ending Gendered Violence—Final Report and Recommendations to Wilfrid Laurier University.*

32 See Mary P. Koss, Jay K. Wilgus, and Kaaren M. Williamsen, "Campus Sexual Misconduct: Restorative Justice Approaches to Enhance Compliance with Title IX Guidance," *Trauma, Violence, & Abuse* 15, no. 3 (2014): 242–257.

33 Rupert Ross, *Returning to the Teachings: Exploring Aboriginal Justice* (Toronto: Penguin Canada, 1996); Christine Sivell-Ferri, *The Four Circles of Hollow Water* (Ottawa: Ministry of the Solicitor General, Ottawa, 1997): 96.

34 See Truth and Reconciliation Commission of Canada, "About the Commission: Indian Residential Schools Truth and Reconciliation Commission," http://trc.ca/websites/trcinstitution/index.php?p=39.

# Endnotes

[35] The Truth and Reconciliation Commission of Canada, *They Came for the Children: Canada, Aboriginal Peoples, and Residential Schools* (Winnipeg: Truth and Reconciliation Commission of Canada, 2012): 79.

[36] Ross, *Returning to the Teachings*, 46.

[37] Sivell-Ferri, *The Four Circles of Hollow Water*, vii.

[38] Sivell-Ferri, *The Four Circles of Hollow Water*, 18.

[39] Community Holistic Circle Healing (CHCH), *CHCH Position Paper on Incarceration*, CHCH file 93.04.20 (Hollow Water: CHCH, 1993): 5, quoted in Sivell-Ferri, *The Four Circles of Hollow Water*, 101.

[40] Sivell-Ferri, *The Four Circles of Hollow Water*, 131.

[41] Sivell-Ferri, *The Four Circles of Hollow Water*, 185.

[42] Joe Couture, Ted Parker, Ruth Couture, and Patti Laboucane, *A Cost-Benefit Analysis of Hollow Water's Community Holistic Circle Healing Process*, APC 20 CA (Ottawa: Aboriginal Corrections Policy Unit, Solicitor General of Canada, 2001).

[43] Couture et al., *A Cost-Benefit Analysis of Hollow Water's Community Holistic Circle Healing Process.*

[44] Sivell-Ferri, *The Four Circles of Hollow Water*, 59.

[45] Howard Sapers, *Annual Report of the Office of the Correctional Investigator 2012–2013* (Ottawa: Office of the Correctional Investigator, 2013), http://www.oci-bec.gc.ca/cnt/rpt/annrpt/annrpt20122013-eng.aspx.

[46] Katherine Van Wormer, "Restorative Justice as Social Justice for Victims of Gendered Violence: A Standpoint Feminist Perspective," *Social Work* 54, no. 2 (2009): 107–116.

[47] To learn more about New Zealand's approach to restorative justice, see Allan MacRae and Howard Zehr, *The Little Book of Family Group Conferences New Zealand Style: A Hopeful Approach When Youth Cause Harm.* (Intercourse: Good Books, 2004).

# About the Authors

**Judah Oudshoorn** is a proud partner to Cheryl and dad to two wonderful children, Emery and Selah. Judah is a Professor in the Community and Criminal Justice program at Conestoga Institute of Technology of Advanced Learning in Kitchener, Canada and a mediator with the Restorative Opportunities program of Correctional Service Canada. He holds a master's degree from the Center for Justice and Peacebuilding (CJP) at Eastern Mennonite University and is a PhD student in Social Work at Wilfrid Laurier University. He has worked for many years with survivors of sexual abuse, people who have offended sexually, as well as families and communities affected by sexual abuse. Judah is the author of the text *Trauma-Informed Youth Justice in Canada* (Canadian Scholars' Press Inc, 2015).

**Lorraine Stutzman Amstutz** works as restorative justice coordinator for Mennonite Central Committee US. She has been involved in the field of restorative justice for many years and co-chaired the international Victim Offender Mediation Association (VOMA) for seven years. She is co-author of *The Little Book of Restorative Discipline for Schools* (Good Books, 2005) and the author of *The Little Book of Victim Offender Conferencing* (Good Books, 2006).

Lorraine speaks and conducts trainings on issues of crime and justice, restorative justice, and conflict transformation. She teaches regularly at CJP's Summer Peacebuilding Institute at Eastern Mennonite University.

**Michelle Jackett** lives with her husband Caleb in Waterloo, Canada. Michelle is the coordinator for the MSCU Centre for Peace Advancement housed at Conrad Grebel University College on the University of Waterloo campus. She is also a lecturer at the University of Waterloo, teaching restorative justice. Michelle earned a master's degree in conflict transformation, specializing in restorative justice, from CJP at Eastern Mennonite University.

# Suggested Readings in *The Little Books of Justice & Peacebuilding* Series

- *The Little Book of Restorative Justice* by Howard Zehr
- *The Little Book of Victim Offender Conferencing* by Lorraine Stutzman Amstutz
- *The Little Book of Circle Processes* by Kay Pranis
- *The Little Book of Trauma Healing* by Carolyn Yoder
- *The Little Book of Family Group Conferences* by Allan Mac-Rae & Howard Zehr
- *The Little Book of Restorative Justice for People in Prison* by Barb Toews
- *The Little Book of Restorative Justice for Colleges and Universities* by David Karp
- *The Little Book of Restorative Discipline for Schools* by Lorraine Stutzman Amstutz & Judy H. Mullet

# Other Suggested Readings

- *Sexual Offending and Restoration* by Mark Yantzi (Herald Press, 1998)
- *Trauma and Recovery* by Judith Lewis Herman (Basic Books, 1997)
- *The Four Circles of Hollow Water* by Christine Sivell-Ferri (Ministry of the Solicitor General, 1997)

Group Discounts for

# The Little Book of Restorative Justice for Sexual Abuse
## ORDER FORM

If you would like to order multiple copies of *The Little Book of Restorative Justice for Sexual Abuse* for groups you know or are a part of, please email **bookorders@skyhorsepublishing.com** or fax order to **(212) 643-6819**. (Discounts apply only for more than one copy.)

Photocopy this page and the next as often as you like.

---

### The following discounts apply:

| | |
|---|---|
| 1 copy | $5.99 |
| 2-5 copies | $5.39 each (a 10% discount) |
| 6-10 copies | $5.09 each (a 15% discount) |
| 11-20 copies | $4.79 each (a 20% discount) |
| 21-99 copies | $4.19 each (a 30% discount) |
| 100 or more | $3.59 each (a 40% discount) |

*Free Shipping for orders of 100 or more!*

*Prices subject to change.*

---

*Quantity*                                              *Price*      *Total*

*The Little Book of Restorative*

_____ copies of *Justice for Sexual Abuse* @      _____   _____

(Standard ground shipping costs will be added for orders of less than 100 copies.)

# METHOD OF PAYMENT

❒    Check or Money Order
      (*payable to **Skyhorse Publishing** in U.S. funds*)

❒    Please charge my:
❒ MasterCard ❒ Visa
❒ Discover    ❒ American Express
# _____

Exp. date and sec. code_____

Signature _____

Name _____

Address _____

City_____

State _____

Zip_____

Phone_____

Email _____

SHIP TO: (if different)
Name _____

Address _____

City_____

State _____

Zip_____

Call: (212) 643-6816
Fax: (212) 643-6819
Email: bookorders@skyhorsepublishing.com
(do not email credit card info)